The Search for the Holy

William F. Kraft

Cathedral Publishing
Pittsburgh, Pennsylvania

Cathedral Publishing
Pittsburgh, PA 15260
412-624-6135
http:/www.pitt.edu/~ondemand

ISBN: 1-887969-09-8

Manufactured in the United States of America
Produced on acid-free paper

Library of Congress Cataloging-in-Publication Data

Kraft, William F., 1938–
    The search for the holy / William F. Kraft.
        p.   cm.
    Originally published : Philadelphia : Westminster Press , 1971.
    Includes bibliographical references.
    ISBN 1-887969-09-08 (alk. paper)
    1. Psychology, Religious.   2. Holy , The.   I . Title.
BL53.K7   1999
291.4'2—dc21   98–45956
                                                                    CIP

—For Patty

Preface to 1971 Edition

My reason for writing this book has its origin in my ambiguous feelings and questions about the meaning of God. Theories and explanations of the holy experience support both the idea of a Supreme Being and the idea that God is a projection of oneself. Both of these ideas are difficult to relate to—for me and, I believe, for many others. I want to experience a God whose impact on my life is both significant and lasting.

This yearning to experience a God often emerges, for example, in psychotherapy. I find that many people who are fighting unconscious conflicts are also desperately trying to make sense of their lives. Their loneliness, depression, anxiety, and frustration repeatedly manifest an absence of a basic presence. I see many others struggling to find a reason for being and, although many are successful and affluent, most of them are leading adequate, but meaningless lives. They are normal in the ordinary, accepted sense of normalcy. I am convinced, however, that they are not what they realistically could be. Their lives are adjusted—accommodated—but are not really happy and meaningful.

I listen to these people in therapy, in groups, in classrooms, in hospitals, and in everyday encounters. I discover that embedded in these struggling personalities is a crucial search for an experience that would make all other experiences at least understandable. I also discover that some emerge from their apparently meaningless experiences to realize a deep and lasting meaning.

Numerous experiences in this realm evoked in me a desire for more research based on these kinds of questions: What is the meaning of this struggle? Is this pain simply a symptom of maladjustment, or can it be an indication of growth? Where and how do I find meaning that makes sense even of apparent non-sense? Is this an experience of the Holy? If so, how and why does the holy experience occur? How and why does it not occur? What difference does it make? These are some of the questions I will investigate thoroughly and hope to answer in the following pages. My professional bias will be psychology, and my approach will be primarily phenomenological-existential.

Before I proceed with these investigations, I should like to thank some of the people who assisted me. Particular gratitude is due to Adrian van Kaam, my mentor, and to Bernard Boelen and Bert van Croonenberg for their personal and professional concern. I am also grateful to Regis Ebner and Clare McKeever for their editorial comments and to Lila Gould and Sylvia Lencyzk for their secretarial assistance. Finally, I thank my parents, on whose shoulders I stand, and my wife for her constructive criticism and supportive love.

—William F. Kraft

Preface to the 1999 Edition

The Search for the Holy was a response to the questions of a young seeker of truth. Now, as a middle-aged pilgrim, I strive more than ever to make sense of our reason for being. During my adult journey, I have written many more books and articles in response to those original questions. So, why is this book reprinted?

Readers assured me that the book is still seminal and relevant to present times—that it helps them make sense of their ultimate questions. They also thought that a reprint could affirm and unite the common vision and experiences that we all share regardless of age.

Nevertheless, a reprint does have limits. Thirty years of new or at least expanded thinking would not be incorporated. Speaking out of my ambivalence, how would a rewrite differ from a reprint?

Although exclusive language was used "back then," it is distracting and unjust. I would rewrite with inclusive language. Fortunately, while remaining faithful to the book's original style, I did change most of the sexist language to more androgynous prose. Along with deleting a few out-dated examples, these language changes were the only modifications made; otherwise, the book remains as the original.

Because of personal as well as cultural and scientific developments, a rewritten book would be more explicitly spiritual. The sixties and seventies ushered in a movement of "self"-actualization, esteem, liberation, encounter, individuation, confrontation, expression, salvation. Individualism was (and still is) paramount. Spiritual movements that went beyond self, like 12-step programs, were not known as they are now.

Furthermore, the "spiritual" had no place in the house of psychology. To write about the spiritual as an integral dynamic in being healthy was inadmissible. Thus, the word "self" was used euphemistically for "spirit." Similarly, since there was no room for God or even a Higher Power/Care, "holy other" was a viable substitute. Now the social sciences and culture are beginning to be more open to the spiritual dimension. A new draft would include more explicit and extensive descriptions and explanations of the spiritual life and of God and God's influence.

I would also be inclined to modify some of the age ranges for the experiences of no-thingness. For instance, I would distinguish between mid-life and middle age as well as explore more extensively the elderly years. Furthermore, displacements of God/the Holy would include addictions and co-addictions. Addictive disorders can be construed as attempts to replace God as our saving and healing experience that leads to freedom and serenity. In fact, only God (not self and our addictive and co-addictive behaviors) can restore us to sanity. Although I knew nothing about 12-step programs when I wrote *The Search for the Holy*, the book is amazingly congruent with the structure and dynamics of addiction and recovery.

Love, a key concept in the book, tends to be codependent. My vision of love was oriented too much around the welfare of others at the expense of responsible self-love. Such love was symptomatic of a sincere and naive idealist. My present focus is not on the "other" or on "self," but rather on "us" —self-others —God.

To foster the welfare of community would be the operative approach.

Finally, few if any deletions would be made in the bibliography, for the books included then speak to me now. But I would add some new works that address our search or the Holy. In short, although I would modify and polish the original manuscript, the vision of a young man still stands and guides the life of an older man.

When I wrote this book, I was a husband but not a father; now I am also a father of two adult children. *Tempus fugit.* I thank my family for letting me be part of them. I thank my friends and mentors, past and present, they will always form and inform me. Special thanks are given to Frank Lehner and Virginia Buckwalter of Cathedral publishing. Frank invited, encouraged, and helped me to reprint this book. Virginia's diligent deciphering and typing implemented our project. Finally, I thank my original and ultimate Source of Being, to whom I journey closer.

—William F. Kraft

Contents

1 A Theory of Self

TO APPRECIATE my experience of the Holy I must understand myself. The search for God is also a search for self and the search for self includes the discovery of God. This re-search begins with oneself.

THE SPIRIT

I, being human, interact in many ways. My most intimate and fulfilling interaction is my spiritual presence to reality. For example, my spiritual experience of a sunset differs radically from an everyday and work experience of a sunset. Usually I take a sunset for granted, or I may curiously analyze it. In my spiritual dimension, however, I experience an uncanny feeling of being one with the sunset—in a sense I am the sunset. I do little, if any, thinking in my purest moments; my experience automatically excludes rational analysis in favor of intimacy and self-surrender. In this beautiful encounter I am willing to obey and follow the mystery of reality, and in my awesome reverence I experience a certain kinship with nature. Although I am totally involved, I know intuitively that I am most uniquely me, that my own singularity stands out in clear relief.

This experience also incorporates a mysterious and paradoxical encounter with the sunset wherein I am able to experience joy and dread, to be proud and humble, to feel freely dependent, and to feel significantly insignificant. I may feel confident and strong, free and independent, yet I may also feel very small. I may also experience myself as being out of my body and yet one with my body. I experience myself as being one with the universe and as a

17

very limited part of an unlimited whole.

My spiritual experience also includes a concrete and ecstatic transcendence. This does not mean that I escape into fantasy, but that I experience reality in a different way. I move beyond my usual modes of interaction and I surrender myself to a reality that is more than me. I experience that everything and everyone are interwoven threads of the same tapestry. In this transcendent encounter I feel that I am one with the sunset. Even though I may have many problems, my transcendence enables me to experience the fundamental unity in life, and in this way, I go beyond my limits. Transcendence offers me a richer appreciation of life that can even bring new meaning to the limits of everyday living. I experience my individuality and my limits as being part of living and as a challenging avenue to its deeper dimensions.

Another way to look at a person as spiritual is in terms of our interpersonal relationships. I, as spirit, have a respectful reverence for another person. I have the propensity to give to—and to be one with—you. I have no need to manipulate or dominate you, nor do I need to seduce you to satisfy my own needs. I am not seduced by your sensuality, nor do I analyze you. In my spiritual dimension I take a second look at, or respect, the uniqueness of you. I feel a spontaneous and centrifugal inclination to accept, affirm, and understand you.

In love, the most fundamental and highest form of spiritual interaction, I reveal and offer the most intimate dimension of my being—my spiritual self. I am most uniquely and personally me in love. I take off my everyday masks to be myself-for-the-other. I paradoxically feel most myself in the very act of giving myself, and I begin to see differently because new possibilities emerge on my horizon of love. In love I give myself to and for our sake, for

I desire to promote our happiness and welfare. My availability-for-the-other is end-centered in that it is a pure giving and not a means toward another end. In love I give myself unconditionally. I love you for what and who you are. My love does not depend on how you behave.

In love I also reveal my most vulnerable aspect—my spiritual self. Although I gain my deepest strength in love, the pain received in love is most penetrating. Thus, when I am hurt in love I may be very reluctant to reveal myself again, or I may look for certain guarantees that I will not be hurt again. Unfortunately, some people may go through their lifetimes seeking these guarantees and consequently never risking themselves in love. If everyone is waiting for the guarantee of not being hurt, then no one may extend the risky invitation to another in love. Thus, we arrive at the tragic situation wherein a person lives and dies with the frustrating wish that someone else will take the first step. A lover, who is willing to suffer for the other's sake, finds that pain in love makes sense.

My spiritual dimension is also critical for our interpersonal life. For instance, my most fundamental and long-range decisions are usually a result of my "transrational" self processes, not a result of a conscious, planned, and analytical process. In our spiritual dimension, we opt for a basic orientation—to be open or closed toward significant experiences or situations. When we fall in love, we do not systematically gather knowledge about our possible beloved, analyze the data, and then decide whether or not to love. Love is not this cold and calculating. On the contrary, love transcends rational analysis to a level of self-surrender. Love is a mysterious happening. We find ourselves in love; we do not put ourselves in love. Our decision is not to like this or that attribute of another, but we see these qualities in the light of love. Our decision of love enables us to love ourselves and others regardless of desirable or undesirable attributes.

When our main motivation is spiritual, we live an orientation of openness and love. We become dynamic discoverers who are constantly uncovering reality and growing into its mystery. We become more and more in tune with reality by openly admitting our experiences.

Our option to make discovery our life project means that we grow in the celebration of life. In the following analyses we will consider some significant experiences and functions of a person who lives primarily according to his or her spirit.

Authority and Obedience

In my spiritual dimension, I experience an inner freedom and responsibility wherein I am the author and origin of my acts. I experience my most fundamental authority. Such personal authority comes from within me and serves as the basis of the various kinds of authority that I receive from my functions in life. The authority I *am* acts as the foundation for the authority I *have*. For example, if a teacher is not the authentic author of her life, her role authority will be an intrusive technique that elicits disrespect and resentment. Her functional authority, without personal authority, will breed discontent. Fundamentally, a *person*, not a role, commands respect and obedience.

Paradoxically, personal authority is achieved primarily through obedience to myself and the Other. (Here the term "Other" refers to persons and the Holy.) Obedience means to listen to the sense in a situation. When I listen I can begin to discover the truth. True obedience must begin with myself, and when I can listen to my own truth, the truth of the Other will begin to resonate within me. Thus, I can be truly obedient to others only if I am obedient to myself. My obedience will liberate me at least in becoming more sensitive in differentiating truth from fiction. Too often, however, I hear only what I want to hear. I hear only what fits into my frames of reference. For example, when someone tells me something I am inclined to accept only those views which support my own. To listen openly means that I must temporarily suspend my own point of view in favor of the other person's viewpoint. Only then can I understand what the person is really saying. The art of obeying involves the ability to shut up and really listen to what is being said.

Obedience and authority are mutually implicated. The true authority obeys and acts on the sense in self and in others. The more we listen, the more we are capable of making a good decision. Furthermore, our respectful listening will appeal to others to listen to and consequently obey us. Likewise, being truly obedient persons we learn to be the author of our existence. Our listening helps us to determine ourselves by opening us to the emergence of reality. We become an authority on living our life by listening to it.

Autonomy

Although autonomy is not the exclusive domain of the spirit, it is another of its important functions. The etymology of autonomy—the Greek *autos* (same, self) and *nomos* (law)—points to the fundamental reality of autonomy. Autonomous persons live according to internal convictions. Our "laws" are in tune with ourselves. When I authentically actualize myself, the main motivating force of my life comes from within. I realize that although I depend on others, only I can live my life. Yet, my autonomy also means that I can freely choose to be dependent.

My self independence also enables me to transcend many everyday problems and to discover deeper meaning in reality. I am not so conditioned by the environment that I react automatically, but I am free to experience many meanings in the same situation. For example, a person's hostility does not automatically evoke hostility in me. His hostility may mean that he is hurt or frightened, that I am hostile toward him, that he learned to be hostile to survive, or that he hates himself.

Freedom

We can also consider freedom to be primarily a function of the spiritual self in several ways. First, the most fundamental form of freedom is freedom-to-be, or self-determination. As a free person I determine my life insofar as my openness enables me to say yes or no to realities. My freedom-to-be also means that since I commit myself to grow progressively deeper into reality, my field of possibilities expands; I experience more possibilities in my situation. My liberating growth demands commitment, for my life necessitates that I be in tune with and love others. I must be open and caring in order to be free.

Freedom also implies a lack of restraint, and in this sense freedom is a *freedom-from*. Determining myself, I am unlikely to be seduced by the immediacy of the world. I am not completely bound by my situation. Although my environment may offer me few opportunities, I am free to transcend and acquire deeper meaning in my constricted environment. For example, a "free" prisoner might find deeper meaning in a concentration camp than a person imprisoned in opulence.

Furthermore, my freedom is limited. For instance, my decision for something excludes many other things. A person who opts for celibacy cannot be the same witness to marriage as can the married person, an option to live in the United States excludes living in Europe, and an option to love lessens hate. The limits of my body or the body-at-large—the world—are also incorporated in freedom. Since my freedom is embodied, I am never completely free. However, being free, I am well aware of my limits, and my knowledge helps me to transcend them. Being limited, my freedom calls for discipline. I am disciplined when I am a disciple or follower of reality. My disciplined presence to reality enables me to admit what is happening; I can freely say yes or no to my experience. For example, when I can be open to my unwanted inclinations, not only am I liberating myself from the immature or unhealthy shackles of repression but I also gain a creative control and sense of my desires. This is discipline and freedom.

My freedom also influences my everyday behavior. I am able to express and to share myself in a more flexible and disciplined way. My thinking also becomes more flexible. I am free enough to consider many points of view, and am not bound merely by my own viewpoint. I become an inner-directed person who is a witness to a free life.

Faith

Faith is essentially linked with acceptance. When I opt to be open to my experience, I accept (*ad-cipere* = to take in) or admit (*ad-mittere* = to send toward) my experiences. It can be said that I "own up to them." When I admit (to) my experiences I affirm them and "let them in" to my being. Acceptance also promotes responsibility in that I am able to respond to situations more openly.

In this psychological context we define faith as a creative acceptance or admittance of experiences that cannot be explained. Although some of my experiences are inexplicable, they are nevertheless real and are known by me pre-reflectively. Faith involves a dynamic and affirmative incorporation of the mystery of reality. Faith is not speculation wherein I reflect on the possibilities of a situation. Neither is faith a type of magical thinking wherein I make reality be what I want it to be, nor is my faith a rationalization used to justify something that I do not experience. My faith is an affirmation and incorporation of my experience, not a means of reinforcing fantasy.

Faith is always, and necessarily, faith *in* something, because faith is a response (of acceptance) to a call of reality. This appeal from reality is not faith, but faith is my open response to the mystery of reality. Thus, the main impetus of faith comes from within me. In faith I accept (faith) or reject (bad faith) my experience. When I opt to accept the mystery of life, I affirm and validate my experience. Furthermore, my yes to reality incorporates a commitment to what I have faith in. Faith means that I will continue to follow reality and consequently become a disciple of mystery.

I have faith not only in the holy Other but also in myself. Much of my experience cannot be explained but should be accepted. To be healthy I must promote a dynamic presence to my own experience, for without this faith in myself I will know almost nothing. Finally, faith in myself is a necessary condition for faith in another. I must accept that which I experience before I can accept that which another experiences. How can I accept the mystery of another if I am not open to my own mystery?

Gordon Allport states that a person who is authentically faithful must come to a "heuristic belief"—one that is never absolutely sure but grows in degrees of probability (*The Individual and His Religion*, pp. 72-74). Although an absolute faith may give a temporary sense of false security in knowing all the answers, this faith robs reality of its mystery and will eventually disintegrate. Absolute certainty is, moreover, inauthentic and impossible because it is against the emergent nature of reality. Authentic faith is a matter of personal development, not a matter of having a method to justify the unknown. A faithful person grows in degrees of certitude and progressively opens up to new horizons.

We can see that faith and openness are dialectically related. Faith presupposes the option of openness because I can only accept the mystery that I am open to, and my faith moves me to accept and witness to that mystery. If I do not affirm and incorporate mystery, my openness will become a fantasy. Thus, a faithful person is open to and is a living witness to the mystery of reality.

THE EGO

My ego mode of existence is oriented to the worlds of work, science, and task-oriented behavior in general. For example, most workers must be relatively impersonal in contrast to their more personal self modes of interaction. Think of how a businessman behaves in his work situation; his behavior is mainly task-oriented. He has a job to do and his main concern is to come to grips with the demands of his task in a practical and efficient way. His business life usually demands that he think and act in a purposeful and logical way. Since management, organization, and control are important, he often operates on a quasi-scientific and technical level. He is constantly solving "problems"—issues that must be settled or proved true or false.

The surgeon, for example, is necessarily task-oriented and impersonal in his surgery. Purely personal behavior would be inappropriate. The surgeon must be exact and precise in the technique of her profession. She should know, as much as humanly possible, what is and what will occur; she must be in control of the situation. Although a patient wants to be treated with personal care in the pre- and post-operative periods, he would be incensed if the surgeon would take a personal therapeutic approach during the operation. The patient expects that the surgeon will be cold, efficient, and manipulative while operating on him.

Or, it is absurd for a plumber to be personally intimate when repairing a clogged drain. It is equally ridiculous for a mother to maintain a playful attitude when her child gets hurt. She must take charge, put her feelings aside, size up the situation, and act to solve the problem. Her behavior may be motivated by and permeated with love, but her actions to help her child must be efficient and task-oriented.

We can see that in my ego interaction I take a conscious distance from a situation, which makes for clear thinking and impersonal involvement. My ego presence to reality is precise and definitive. It is not immediate, private, or impulsive as the interaction of my body, nor is it paradoxical, ineffable, direct, and universal as my spiritual presence, but my ego interaction is clear, mediate, public, and abstract. My ego presence is also oriented to the common world—the world of common discourse. For example, when I use ego language I am exposing myself to the public and am inviting criticism. Most ego language is open to all; it is not intimate or private. Public systems of communication, especially verbal speech, depend on ego processes, and without the ego, nothing could be written, built, or verbally spoken. In short, in my ego dimension I deal more with the clear and public as contrasted with the paradoxical and unique of the spiritual self.

My ego functions primarily in terms of reflective thinking and willing. I reflect rationally on a situation, think about it, and then make a decision. I attack reality in terms of a problem-solving situation and I am in control of what I am doing. However, a difficulty arises when I reflect on my experience, because my experience can never be exactly reflected or thought out in exact terms. My immediate experience is always more than my mediated ego knowledge. Even though ego communication is always inadequate, especially with intimate experiences, it is very valuable and necessary. Ego discourse promotes explicit sharing of experiences, as in speaking and writing, and it enables me to gain more control, clarification, and insight into my experience.

People as ego can be considered to be managers. Every person is a manager in some area of his or her intra- and extra-psychic life. A homemaker must manage household chores; the business-woman manages her work and personnel; we must manage finances; the student must manage her studies. A person must also manage to act appropriately in situations, manage to think correctly, manage space and time, manage to make sense, and manage oneself. Management connotes control of a situation as a means of meeting certain goals wherein I manage to organize reality in a task-oriented manner. I more or less calculate, plan, and consciously put things into place. For instance, I reflect on my feelings, moods, thoughts, and standards, and try to make explicit sense of them. The numerous demands and possibilities of my world must also be put in order; otherwise, my life becomes a chaos. Finally, I strive for a balanced integration between the internal and the external dimensions of my life.

In an ego mode of existence I am capable of detaching myself from a situation to protect myself or to take a second look at myself. I am not likely to follow blindly the loudest and most articulate voice. Neither will I be prone to be seduced by group hysteria. Nor will I tend to act impulsively when under pressure. By dealing with and coping with the situation at hand, I do not become inappropriately involved, but I realistically meet the demands of my situation.

Finally, my ego enables me to practice what I preach. My creative self-insights remain in my mind and do not affect the world unless they are implemented by my ego. Ideas may come easily, but the execution of ideas takes much ego work in the forms of thinking, decision-making, planning, analyzing, organizing, and problem-solving. Ideally, I should strive for a harmony between my spiritual and ego processes. Without the creativity of my spiritual self, my ego functions become useless means and frequently become ends in themselves, and I soon become an efficient barbarian. Without the functions of my ego, my spiritual self becomes a seductive fantasy often resulting in a schizoid mode of living.

THE BODY

Our psychological body refers to our third primary presence to reality—the body that interacts in the world with others. This body is not the body of medicine, physiology, or biochemistry; it is my body which I live.

My lived-body also has distinctive functions which differ from those of my ego and spirit. For instance, a person who drives an automobile usually does not think to increase speed, brake, steer, or find directions. He trusts his pre-reflective knowledge of driving and seldom gives it a thought. He usually thinks about his driving only if something goes wrong. His body—hands, arms, legs, eyes, ears, etc.—knows how to drive. If he had to reason every operation, the effort and tension would exhaust him and impede the smooth flow of his driving. Neither does this person have an intimate and transcendent encounter, for such behavior would be simply inappropriate and probably would cause an accident.

Likewise, the fingers of the violinist know the concerto better than her ego. In fact, if during a performance she were to take time to reflect, her music would become noise. The fingers of the typist also know the keys better than her ego, so that when the typist begins to think, she usually makes mistakes or slows up. In the same way the athlete cannot afford to think when playing the game. This is what time-outs are for. Finally, a person's spontaneous body knowledge and language in sexuality may be truer and less inhibiting than those of the ego. When we begin to think in sexual dialogue, we become once removed from the situation. The ultimate of sexuality is to let myself know the other without the impurities of thinking.

My bodily interaction with reality is immediate and pre-reflective, and my knowledge is, at least initially, implicit and undifferentiated. For example, my bodily feelings seldom lie, for they are in direct and pure contact with the world. However, the knowledge of my feelings is ambiguous and equivocal and it tends to intermingle with the knowledge of my other feelings. It behooves me to be openly present to the messages of my body and then periodically to think about them. This thinking is important because it enables my ambiguous body knowledge to become clear and distinct. I must remember, however, that (ego) thinking about my feelings is fruitless without a prior and necessary (spiritual) openness to them.

Rooting me in the world and anchoring me to the earth, my body draws the world into me. For instance, my senses bring the world to me in their various modalities. Since I and another necessarily express ourselves in and through our bodies, we can know each other. My body makes me and another present and accessible to each other. Without my body, I am no-where, no-one, and no-body.

The density and demands of my body are also constant reminders of my embeddedness in the world. My body prevents me from living exclusively in a mental world. Because I am an embodied person, I must live the fundamental structures of reality. I must eat, sleep, be sheltered, live in time and space, and contact the world through the structures of my senses and nervous system. If I abuse these structures, I will pay the price. If I eat too much, I get fat. If I do not eat enough, I become weak. If I refuse to follow these rules, I will die physically or psychologically. Indeed, although I must obey these rules, I am marginally free in regard to their particular execution.

I—as embodied psyche—am also structured in that I can make contact only through perspective. My bodily modalities of the senses, movements, and postures let me see the world in and through perspective, and consequently I can reach the Other only in limited ways. Even though my self enables me to be a horizon of possibilities, my body forces me to actualize only a few of them.

Finally, my body is impulsive and selfish without the meditative thought of my ego or the respect of my spirit. My body in itself strives for immediate relief and will blindly use anything or anybody to achieve its pleasure. This kind of bodily existence is exclusive of the Other in that it acts only on behalf of its own interests. Although my body puts me in the world and enables me to contact the Other, my body needs my ego and my spirit to become truly human.

CONCLUSIONS

Everyday Behavior

My usual or everyday behavior normally calls for body and/or ego modes of interaction, while my spiritual self is not directly expressed. For instance, a homemaker's behavior does not usually call for spiritual interaction. Expression of her spiritual self while cleaning the house or changing diapers would be inappropriate behavior. However, her spirit can be implicitly present or absent. If she represses her spirit, her everyday behavior becomes merely functional and without significant purpose, resulting in boredom. If her spirit influences her everyday ego and body interaction, her routine will be permeated with transcendent purpose. If her spirit is present and expressed explicitly in appropriate situations, her routine living and work will be made easier and more meaningful. Her spiritual experiences will have the effect of liberating her in all modes of behavior—including her work. Furthermore, if her everyday life should change, as with the unexpected appearance of her husband or with loving demands from her children, she is ready to express herself overtly in love.

Such self experiences as love, however, have been relegated to certain situations and to particular times. This is usually valid, for we cannot always be loving overtly. Love is too intense to be constantly explicit and, besides, most situations do not call for such love. However, it is very important to realize that we can always express our love implicitly in that all our behavior can be performed in the context of love. We can live with an orientation of love. For example, a teacher who acts merely on an ego level lacks conviction, and his students experience him as efficiently boring. He can also stand out on an ego and bodily level, which he usually must do, within the context of self spontaneity and concern. Although he may express his self directly, if it is appropriate, his spiritual self usually forms the background for the foreground of his body and ego functions. Pupils experience this teacher as a genuine, open, and concerned educator. This situation is conducive to learning.

Likewise, the nurse who operates only on an ego level is an efficient though poor nurse. Authentic nursing incorporates both self and ego functions. A nurse's spirit, although usually implicit, humanizes the nursing techniques. We can say that nursing techniques without concern are cold and make for efficient robots, but that techniques used in the context of love and as implementations of care make for warm and therapeutic nurses. Patients experience authentic nurses as trained persons who really care.

My body is also in tune with love at least insofar as I must "express" my love as a man or as a woman. My authentic love is always incarnated in this sexual way. However, romantic love is intensely embedded in the emotions and is therefore experienced as intensely real. Love expressed in genital sexuality explicitly incorporates both body and spirit, resulting in the unique unity of self transcendency and bodily pleasure.

Beauty

Beauty is a mode of behavior that involves a harmony of the spirit, ego, and body with the spiritual self as the main dynamic force. As in music, my transcendent joy and immediate pleasure are embedded within a certain framework—a framework that is bounded by ego technique. Thus, when I enjoy a symphony I experience a transcendent and pleasurable truth within the context of the musical framework and virtuosity. My experience of beauty in nature, such as of a sunset, is fundamentally the same as a work of art. Although the form or mode of expression is not humanly made, the form still exists. Thus, in an aesthetic experience I enjoy letting my whole being be.

Play

One of the most interesting and fascinating kinds of behavior is play. A significant factor in play is that it incorporates certain structures and/or rules that safeguard me from being hurt. Since I and another know, consciously or unconsciously, the structure of our play situation, we can afford to be at ease. We do not have to hide or to be phony. Although my play is not usually as intimate as my love, I do experience a freedom to be myself with a minimum risk of being hurt.

Play is ordinarily an interpersonal relationship. Even when I play by myself, another is usually present in my fantasy. However, my main intention is not to give to others, as in love, but simply to express, which may involve giving. Thus, play is more a question of being and expression that bring a sense of well-being. We can simply be ourselves.

My play differs radically from my customary activity. I take time out from my everyday and work worlds to recreate and play.

Since play is a creative retreat from my everyday worlds of tension, play is a pretension. It comes before and after the tension of ordinary living.

Any mode of presence can be accented in play. For example, a child's play is centered on the body and frequently serves as an avenue for the ego to explore reality. Sexual play allows a person to express directly through the immediacy of body. Intellectual games offer ego functions an added degree of free expression. Play in the spiritual dimension is my deepest mode of dwelling in and being with the world. To play with another in love, to feast with friends, to dwell in nature, and to laugh at myself are all modes of playful celebration.

Person and Personality

Finally, we can consider the terms "person" and "personality" in the light of our framework. The etymology of person means an actor's mask or a character in a play. Mask need not be used in the sense of hiding from the world, but used as a particular mode of facing the world. To be a person, one must interact in the spirit, ego, or bodily modes of presence. Thus, only a human can be a person. Infants, for instance, are persons because they interact with their environment, although explicitly only on a bodily level. Neurotics, who attempt to reject some of their experiences, are nevertheless persons because they are involved in the world, although in a relatively closed manner. Likewise, one who is mentally retarded is a person; the same is true for a psychotic person. Thus, all people—of all ages, degrees of health and intelligence, races, cultures, etc.— should be respected as persons.

We define personality as a dynamic gestalt of a person's actual modes of experience. Therefore, personality presupposes the person and is determined by the person and other factors, such as genetic endowment, environment, culture, temperament, and interpersonal relationships. A person's personality is always unique, for it incorporates the unique quality and degree of his or her physical, functional, and spiritual actualization. A child, for instance, has a personality, but it is not as matured as a healthy adult's. It may also be said that one person has a dynamic personality and another has a lethargic personality. However, since person and personality are not synonymous, a person may have a rather dead personality and still be a healthy person. On the other hand, a person may have a dynamic personality and be rather unhealthy. The healthy person, however, usually has an appealing and comforting personality.

2 Our Experience of the Holy

MY RE-SEARCH for the holy experience took me in many directions. I read the literature on God. The mystics and spiritual writers offered me personal insights into the experience of God, and the scholars gave me reasons for and against the existence of God. In my work with small groups people frequently expressed a genuine concern for the relevance of God. Openly expressing ourselves, we found that each person's experience of God differed somewhat from another's. We realized that such factors as religion, ethnic background, constitution, personal history, education, and maturity influenced our experience of God. Nevertheless, we came to a common ground—a ground that made all our experiences holy.

I also asked people to write spontaneous descriptions about their experience of God. I had them describe a holy experience as openly as possible, without using theories about God. These native descriptions helped me to understand what people mean by a holy experience.

Finally, I listened to individuals in counseling and in friendly dialogue. I realized that although people used various terms in talking of this holy experience, such as God, Absolute Thou, Personal Transcendent, ultimate concern, and religious and mystical experience, all were pointing to the same reality. I also listened to my own holy experiences and tried to explicate what happened. The goal of the following analyses is to present the common factors of these direct and indirect experiences of the Holy while remaining faithful to each experience.

MYSTERY AND PARADOX

Like all my spiritual experiences, my holy experience incorporates mystery and paradox. My mysterious encounter with the Holy points to an ineffable and unusual quality that transcends my normal behavior of ego problem-solving and immediate body satisfaction. Although my holy experience can be pointed to and described partially with words, usually best in poetic and mystical terms, my experience does not lend itself to exact communication. My knowledge of the Holy is so intimate and so beyond my everyday modes of interaction that it becomes extremely difficult to talk about this experience or to reason with it. I face a danger in attempting to become too exact in analyzing my holy experiences. Such certainty can lead to reification, sterilization, and a tendency toward falsification of my holy experience. On the other hand, I must remember that although my paradoxical holy experience is beyond the level of ego analysis, it nevertheless points to a lived and undeniable experience. A refusal to look at my holy experience could become a denial of reality whether my denial is done in the name of scientism or spiritualism.

Experiences of the Holy are also paradoxical, and consequently they seem contradictory or meaningless from a logical perspective. My paradoxical presence to the Holy is a-logical, a-contradictory, and a-discursive. My uncanny and strangely attractive experience is beyond my normal world of dichotomies, either/or, problems, analysis, and distances, for in my holy experience I surrender myself to unity, both/and, mystery, synthesis, and closeness. In my holy encounters I experience the unity of joy and anxiety, attraction and respectful distance, fascination and trepidation, familiarity and mystery, pride and humility. I realize immediately that my sacred experience is related integrally with the profane. My sacred stance becomes profane because I am more deeply in the world, and my profane stance becomes sacred because my world is made holy. Thus, in and through my holy transcendence, I spontaneously take up a new and deeper kinship with the world.

DEPENDENCE

My experience of the Holy demands that I give myself to the holy Other. I depend on the Holy because I need the Holy to love the Holy. In fact, although I need the Holy to exist, my acceptance of this divine dependence makes me free and independent. To be a holy person means that I choose to promote the human and holy Other in my life and thereby gain a new independence and freedom.

I realize that since I cannot force the holy reality to reveal itself and to respond to me, I must depend on the Holy. However, although I can never force the spirit of holiness to encounter me, I can take the initiative to be available when God reveals God's self to me. I also acknowledge that the human (people) and holy (God) Other is a greater and holier reality than myself, and consequently I tend to give a spontaneous respect to the transcendent Other. I find that the Other is overwhelming in reference to me. I know that the human and holy Other is the ground of my existence and that only the Other can fill me with life. Thus, I slowly come to realize that my holy dependence means that the human and holy Other is the ground of my being. A denial of this condition means that I would lose my ground and progressively lead a meaningless life. Finally, I humbly acknowledge that the Holy also depends on me in that the Holy manifests itself most meaningfully in and through humanity. Without us the Holy does not exist for us, because we are the loci for the manifestation of the Holy.

My holy dependence differs radically from infantile, immature, and unhealthy modes of dependency. For instance, since an infant's mode of existence is a bodily one, it is necessary for the infant to take constantly and impossible for him or her to give willingly. Thus, if we are immature or regressed, we act in a way similar to the child. Similarly, an unhealthy dependent man centers his life around satisfying his own needs and not also around giving to the others. His dependency forces him to see life only in terms of his own needs. He may be concerned about others, but only for his own welfare and not for their sake. If his needs are unsatisfied, he feels inferior, uneasy, and dependent. This person leads a precarious existence because he compulsively depends on dependency. He cannot choose freely to be authentically dependent on a reality greater than himself. Often this person will put on a front of being independent because it proves to be an efficient way of satisfying his dependency needs without losing face. Or, he will simply be passively dependent, for most people like quiet and dependent persons in small doses. This person's unconscious exploitation of others and of the Holy makes his love a means only to receive love.

Holy and healthy persons own up to their dependency, a dependency that is centered around giving. Recognizing their need to love others, they become dependable: they are available to others. They do not give to others to satisfy a deficiency, but they love the human and holy Other for their sake. It is the right thing to do.

INDEBTEDNESS

In love, I find that I have been thrown into the world with the vocation of being concerned for others. I admit that to be truly alive is to give, and I openly respond to this call. This call to give points to a primordial mood of indebtedness. I feel that I owe myself to the Other, and I realize that I can be a person only with the Other—God and people, who are part of and beyond me.

I also realize that I have a large debt to pay because I owe the Other my existence. My debt is rooted fundamentally in love at least insofar as my parents, friends, and society have enabled me to become myself. Without their love and the acts emergent from their love, I could not have lived, let alone developed into a person. I have been given so much, especially in childhood, that I have a life-debt to pay. I acknowledge that every person is indebted to others for life and that life without others is a fictive life.

Although my body and ego are indebted to others, my primordial mood of indebtedness is oriented around my spirit. My spiritual indebtedness is more critical to life than that of my ego and body. For example, when I receive "something," I usually feel obliged to return something else. If a thing symbolizes the gift of another person, however, it makes the thing more meaningful and personal. The most risky and intimate gift is of myself in love, for this gift calls for the greatest giving, receiving, and returning. I cannot replace this gift with things; I can only reciprocate with the same gift—myself.

I realize that to give myself to the Other is my most demanding and crucial debt. If I and others do not return the gift of ourselves to each other, life and society will degenerate. When people never give of themselves, the culture suffers and becomes a culture of things, not of persons.

I pay my debt to the human and holy Other most basically by loving the Other. The holy Other makes demands on me in terms of appeal, not force, because God simply asks nothing more than love. The purpose of paying my debt is not to receive a reward. That giving is business. If I should demand a return, I would make love a subtle means of mere personal satisfaction instead of a promotion of community. When I use love to get the rewards of wholeness and holiness, I pervert love and become less whole and holy. A true gift is a giving of myself without the demand of a return. Finally, I again come into the paradoxical realm—the more I pay my debt, the more I am in debt, because the more I give to God, the more God returns to me. Thus, my degree of indebtedness is indicative of my degree of holiness.

At times I may experience a peculiar and subtle sense of guilt with my indebtedness. I feel a primordial unrest, an uncanny uneasiness that is never completely eased. My guilt means that I am in a state of not-yetness, that I am always becoming in my holy encounters. Yet, my guilt enables me to give more to God and others and, consequently, to be more of myself. Thus, to be a holy person means that I must live in guilt. I feel guilty in that I am returning so little compared to what I have received and am receiving. I feel that I am not living up to God's call and that I am not actualizing my potential to be one with God and others. My guilt does not stem from a compulsive attempt to be perfect—to be God—so that I suffer neurotic guilt when I am not 100 percent right. On the contrary, my guilt is a living affirmation of my humanity—that my life is unceasingly growing.

WORSHIP

Worship points to the ways in which I respect, affirm, and give to the human and holy Other. The primordial ground and highest form of worship is love. Although my indebtedness and guilt move me to worship, my primary aim is not to pay my debt or to relieve my guilt. I most authentically worship others because I love them. Without love, my worship becomes a childish and often meaningless ritual, and with love, my worship becomes a meaningful implementation of and witness to love. For instance, a mature husband worships his wife simply because she is worthy of worship. He does not make her a pseudo god so that his worship is fictive and egoistic, but his healthy worship means that he accepts and interacts with his wife as herself. He promotes her well-being, her wholeness and holiness, for he helps her to actualize herself in all dimensions, including her holy life. Thus my worship of others need not be idolatrous, because true worship incorporates in some way an encounter with God. I worship because I love; that is, the human and holy Other, being my ultimate concern in life, simply calls for worship.

My authentic worship is not one of a lower subject looking up at a higher subject. This was often the worship of antiquity. Neither do I worship to propitiate a powerful and primitive god. My encounter is not a submission of will. On the contrary, I freely realize that the holy Other—God—is greater than myself and that the power of God is the inviting power of love. My worship is a yes to these realities. My worship also says that I am grateful to the Other—God and people—for making me be, and I give thanks for this gift of life.

Finally, my worship can take many forms: formal and informal, verbal and nonverbal, private and public, and explicit and implicit. For example, I can learn meaningful forms of public worship that have an advantage of incorporating a communal aspect, wherein I can participate in the same form of worship as others, and thereby promote a personal communion with others. I must realize, however, that these types of worship are meaningless and a sham unless they are personalized by me. Furthermore, although these avenues of worshipping are very important, I must constantly try to discover new ways of worshipping. For instance, I may discover that love is one of my purest forms of worship, or I may find that my everyday life, when lived in the context of love, becomes a subtle yet ever-present worship of God.

FAITH AND DOUBT

Before, during, and after my holy encounters, I experience a paradoxical unity of faith and doubt. My faith incorporates doubt and my doubt incorporates faith. I find that my faith needs doubt in order to develop and that my doubt is the darkness that enables the light of faith to be seen.

We have already seen that the spiritual function of faith is not a question of certainty or exactness but a question of mystery. In and through faith I openly and creatively accept my numinous experiences and thereby grow into the ground of reality. Although my experience is inexplicable, I must admit that I need faith in order to love, because love is beyond the control of the ego and body.

Likewise, I experience doubt in my holy experience in that I am questioning and growing closer to God. I am never certain of God. Certainty would mean that I know everything exactly and thus control everything. In fact, paradoxically, my lack of doubt would mean that I could not trust or risk being open to the mystery of the Other. Such a person lives a fictive life, because a life without doubt exists only in fantasy. Just as disastrous is the person who is in a chronic state of doubt. It is impossible for this person to accept the unsolvable in faith. However, the authentic person is always to some degree in doubt of a transcendent Other. At times, my doubt can become so great that I need faith to make sense out of my experience. At other times, I may achieve a high degree of enlightenment wherein I experience a high degree of certitude. Doubt is needed here so that my holy experience does not become out of tune with the mystery of life. Thus, doubt without faith and faith without doubt are static and inauthentic. The former is a refusal to acknowledge the mystery of life, and the latter is a refusal to accept the risk in living the mystery of life.

My experience of the human and holy Other is a rhythm of light and darkness, faith and doubt. When one is at a high point, the other recedes into the background, ready to manifest itself. Although I may experience a crisis when I am in the throes of doubt, my crisis can serve to promote my future faith. Although my ecstatic joy and enlightenment in faith are to be celebrated, my faith can also help me keep perspective when I am thrown into the darkness of doubt. I must doubt the Holy in order to believe, because my faith accepts that which I can question but cannot reason. I must also believe in order to doubt, because my faith makes available experiences that I can doubt and that consequently become more present to me. Thus, the human and holy Other draws closer and closer to me through the ongoing rhythm of faith and doubt.

TRANSCENDENCE

In my holy encounters, I am involved beyond my usual modes of interaction. I, as spirit, am intimately experience a union with, or being at home in, the mystery of reality. I am not coping with, exploiting, or controlling the Other, but I am in a mode of creative acceptance. I see God and others not in terms of conflict and problems, but in terms of harmony and mystery. This does not mean that I repress real difficulties in my life, but my transcendence enables me to see a more fundamental unity underlying my difficulties. For example, we can experience many pressures in work and homelife, but our transcendence in love enables us to experience a deeper reality that helps us to accept and to cope with the many demands of our lives. This "going beyond" the situation is actually going deeper into the situation through a different stand toward reality. My holy transcendence is to a different world, but not from the world, for in transcendence I am able to see the sacred-profane unity of life—to know and respond to how everything and everyone are interwoven with one another, how we are integral members of the same community.

Thus, my transcendence is not some kind of supernatural or non-human activity, but it is a decidedly human experience. I find that transcendence is not a nebulous dream. It is a concrete and crucial experience. Transcendent experience, however, can be considered abnormal in that most people do not actively promote transcendence in their lives, but try to live only on the ego and body levels, opting for transcendence primarily in times of convenience or need. Too few persons live a life where transcendence is integrated in their total personalities and is a main motivating force in their lives. Thus, although transcendent holy experiences are especially human, they are also frequently outside the norms of contemporary life.

In transcendence, I also have the experience of going beyond my limits. I clearly realize that my limits are still present, but my perspective enables me to see their relatedness with the whole. I can take a respectful distance from them, thereby giving me a certain freedom from them. My affirmation, acceptance, and deeper insight into my limits prevent me from being seduced and shackled by them.

Furthermore, my transcendence in love incorporates a power that is decidedly beyond the willpower of the ego or the strength of the body. The peculiar power of my spiritual transcendence is not concerned primarily with control or expression, but is oriented around a simple presence with, and for, the human and holy Other. In transcendence I experience a strength that is rooted in the core of my being and a confidence that allows me to confront reality more openly. This new ability to respond gives me a solidarity and rootedness, and my positive distance from the trivia of reality enables me to look more clearly at what is happening. Being-with-reality and transcending limits give me power that is rooted primarily in my option to promote the Other as my ultimate concern. My humble obedience to the most powerful force—the human and holy Other—gives me lasting strength. By accepting my powerlessness, I can connect with God's power of love that permeates and goes beyond me.

SACREDNESS

My holy experience can be considered sacred in that God is my ultimate concern. We emphasize the word "ultimate" because all my experiences more or less include concern, but there is only one ultimate concern. In one sense, the ultimate refers to the value that is highest in my hierarchy of values. Every person operates according to a hierarchy of values and each person has an ultimate value—that standard, activity, or object which he or she values most. Sacredness describes what I most revere, respect, love, worship, and base my life on. This value functions as the greatest influence in my life. It is sacred. Of course, our highest value should be in harmony with the ultimate concern of our being—the human and holy Other. (In this context, sacredness points to the "object-pole" of my holy experience as being somewhat more than human, and of evincing such experiences as unity, transcendence, and love.)

The authentic lover always participates explicitly or implicitly in the sacredness of the Other. Although we contend that only the Holy is sacred, I and other persons can be made sacred in Love. Thus, authentic love of another human being is a sacred experience because both of the participants come to experience the holy ground of their love. Their love for each other incorporates the Holy and makes them more available to the Holy, and although the beloved is not the Holy, he or she can become holier in and through love. I come to realize that since every person is oriented toward, and permeated with, the Holy, love for others is a sacred experience.

Ideally, if the center of my life is love of God, all my activities—body, ego, and spirit—will be colored by my holy disposition. This does not mean, however, that I love explicitly in all situations. I still maintain my sphere of interest—work, study, art, play, etc.—although it is implicitly influenced by my concern for the Holy. This is not unusual because our experiences are always influenced by our main motivation in life, no matter what this motivation may be. If a life is centered around work accomplishments, all the facets of that life will be more or less influenced by the central motivation. The same dynamic applies to the holy person, and in this sense all a person's behavior is made holy.

We point out that sacredness is peculiar to the holy experience. An authentic person experiences only the Holy as sacred. Thus, the quality of sacredness is important because it differentiates the holy self experience from other spiritual experiences more than any other factor. Sacredness makes the experience of transcendence holy.

CHARISMATIC RELATIONSHIP

One way that we can consider the holy experience to be charismatic is in terms of its being an interpersonal relationship. My experience of the Holy—with others or in solitude—incorporates a personal transaction between me and the Holy. This interpersonal dimension means that I, primarily as spirit, am involved with another—the Holy—so that I appeal to the Holy or respond to the appeal of the Holy. My interpersonal experience does not mean that the Holy is necessarily a Person, although this may be one of several interpretations of the Holy. However, I as a person experience the Holy, and in this sense the total interpersonal relationship can be called charismatic.

I also experience charisma insofar as I experience a holy presence that draws and appeals to me. Although this holy presence is primarily pre-reflective and numinous, I still experience it intensely. The holy charisma inspires me to transcend myself and to project myself into the Holy. The Holy breathes in a presence that affects me, and although this may sound spiritualistic, it is quite understandable because love does have this effect. The Holy not only appeals to me, but it also responds to my appeal. When I make myself available to the Holy, the Holy may respond in terms of sacred and charismatic love. This love penetrates me with a creative force that induces me to be more whole and holy.

My experience of the Holy can also be considered charismatic in relation to its charismatic effects on me. I gain a charisma in experiencing a creative power that promotes my own personality and inspires others. My power is not the power of ego control, but is the power of spiritual creativity. I become more myself and am able to cut through the roles and facades of normal living to the core of my existence. Through my holy experiences I feel more grounded and at home in the world, and my presence is experienced spontaneously by others. Furthermore, my holy sight into the Other appeals to and encourages others to be more themselves. This holy charisma which occurs in and through love leads us to our next dimension—the way to the Holy.

LOVE

Love is the most direct and intimate way to the Holy for contemporary Western people. In love I open and give myself to the Holy, and I am ready to respond with concern and care for the sake of the Holy. The Holy also loves me in terms of its sacred charisma. The Holy is open to, available to, and gives to me. My love encounters with the Holy occur in three basic ways: in solitude, with another person, and in a group.

My encounter with the Holy in solitude occurs when no other person is explicitly present. I am by myself in my availability to the Holy. I may purposely withdraw from my everyday world to be alone. I may be in the woods, by the sea, in a church, in any room, or doing nothing when I have a holy encounter. In solitude I am in a mode of simplicity. There are few distractions to divert my holy encounter, and my peace and quiet enable me to make myself totally available for the Holy. I do not have to be concerned about other things because my solitude frees me from things in order to be free for the Holy.

Although I am alone with the Holy, other people are present implicitly. My love of the Holy in solitude is also a love of others, because my love in solitude of the holy Other is in implicit affirmation of the human Other. For example, when you encounter the Holy in solitude, you do not directly express love to your friend, for your friend is not directly, but implicitly, present. On the other hand, when you directly express love to a friend, the Holy is implicit in your love. Thus, when one—the human or the holy Other—is explicitly loved, the other is implicitly loved.

I can also love the Holy when I love another person. Here, I explicitly express my love for another person, and in this human love encounter I affirm and love the ground of our beings—the Holy. In my mysterious and transcendent love dialogue, I experience a charismatic reality that promotes a serene unity within and between us and that generates a holy ground which is greater than, yet the basis of, our lives. However, my love of people and of the Holy are not synonymous, because I experience the Holy as different but not separate from others and because I can encounter the Holy directly in solitude. Yet my authentic love for people always includes the Holy, so that love is, at least implicitly, a holy act.

I can also experience the Holy simultaneously and explicitly with another human wherein my love is focused both on another person and on the Holy. For instance, a wife's love may incorporate both her husband and the Holy in the foreground of her experience. Here the wife's love for her beloved and for the Holy are merged, so that the Holy is articulated in the presence of her husband. Although it is quite possible for a person, particularly a woman, to love both man and Holy directly, it is more usual to experience one in the foreground (explicitly) and the other in the background (implicitly).

I can also encounter the Holy in the presence of a group, such as in a liturgical service or in a celebration. My ideal is that people congregate and form a union with one another, and as a loving solidarity we present ourselves to and for the Holy. However, I must remember that although certain liturgical services can promote an encounter with the Holy, it is through love, not through a series of ritualistic acts, that I encounter the Holy.

If I exclude one of these avenues to love the Holy, the other will suffer. If I do not promote my love in solitude, my love of other persons will lose its holiness and therefore its wholeness. In this situation my love of others may progressively regress into a hysterical dependency or a histrionic control. On the other hand, if I try to love the Holy only in solitude, my love will also regress, often into a pietistic narcissism or into a schizoid existence. Our point is that since we are coexistence toward others and toward the Holy, we and the Holy are inseparable in an experience of love. My freedom rests on which object pole—the human or holy Other—I opt to accent.

Furthermore, my love of the Holy is dependent on my own and on my culture's state of development. For example, a primitive person's love of the Holy was probably highly influenced by a dependent and undifferentiated involvement with nature, and in this sense it may have been similar to the child's experience.

Thus, the God of primitive man was probably embedded in the body processes and in nature. Likewise, contemporary dialogue with the Holy is highly influenced by one's personal degree of maturity and by ego-centered culture.

People often ask what is the humanist's relation to the Holy. We can say that humanists, persons who lead a life of authentic love but who do not promote the usual notions of God and religion, experience the Holy implicitly because their openness to and care for other humans in love necessarily incorporates God. Often, however, humanists will eventually be forced to take a stand toward the holy presence in love. They will come to affirm or reject the holy Other in their love. Nevertheless, humanists may not come to this confrontation for a long time or even for a lifetime. Even though their life is not explicitly religious, they do in fact lead a religious or holy life.

People also ask what is the difference between the holy experience and other self experiences. We have seen that holy experiences are self experiences of love. However, I also have other spiritual experiences that do not necessarily incorporate the Holy yet are closely related to holy experiences. For example, I can have an experience of philosophical wonder wherein I have a feeling of seeing in the light of the whole and of being whole myself. I experience a mysterious and transcendent unity with reality, and my experience may promote openness, growth, and fulfillment. However, since my involvement is in being and not in the Holy, sacred charismatic love is really not an issue in my experience. Likewise, my self experience of nature involves beauty, ecstasy, transcendence, paradox, mystery, etc. Again, although I am open to reality and feel whole and fulfilled, I am not necessarily explicitly holy because sacred love, worship, and charisma are not part of my aesthetic experience. However, such self experiences of be-ing and beauty can lead me to or serve as springboards to the Holy, because in being transcendent functions they lend them-selves in the promotion of my holy experiences. Although they can stand on their own in a valid and necessary way, my experi-ence of being and beauty may also transfer into a holy experience. At this point, my experiences are no longer philosophical or aes-thetic but have changed into a holy encounter.

Finally, I may experience being and beauty in terms of or di-rectly with the Holy. For example, I may experience being and beauty in the foreground of my experience, but my implicit pres-ence to the Holy gives my philosophical or aesthetic experience a somewhat different flavor. Beauty, for instance, becomes holy to me insofar as the foreground of my aesthetic experience is perme-ated with the background of my holy experience. I may also experi-ence being or beauty simultaneously with the Holy. For instance, I may experience the mystery of being and at the same time expe-rience the Holy, so that both being and the Holy are in the fore-ground of my experience.

In the light of our analysis of love, we can consider prayer to be our dialogue of love with the Holy. Prayer involves a response to the call of the Holy wherein the Holy invites me to listen to and accept the call to foster the serenity and freedom of being together in Love. Prayer also incorporates my call to the Holy to guide and care for us. Thus, I-God-You form a community of peace.

The language of prayer is not merely verbal. It also has other modes of expression. Prayer is basically a being-with the Holy, and without this presence to and for the Holy, words are mean-ingless. Words might serve to hide the Holy. The kind of language—verbal and nonverbal—depends much upon the situation. Our point is to avoid becoming fixated in one mode of expression but to promote an availability to all possible forms of communication. Many of us know the fruit of prayer with others; we see that our whole life can be a prayer if ultimately oriented to the Holy. The danger, however, is to become so busy that the Holy encountered in solitude is lost. Such a person's compulsion to be involved may exclude the involvement of solitude.

Our final point in this section is that I can be present to the Holy in other ways besides love. Although love is my most direct and intimate way to the Holy, my everyday life can be lived in the context of the Holy, so that all my behavior is in some way congruent with and linked with love—my fundamental motivation in life. I can also contact the Holy intellectually wherein I, as ego, reflect of my immediate experiences. For example, although theology is primarily a reflective and indirect presence to the Holy, it is nevertheless a way of grasping the Holy. However, if the theologian's reflective knowledge about the Holy is not rooted in pre-reflective experience, his intellectual contact will be lifeless, meaningless, and useless. On the other hand, since an ego approach such as theology helps to make the Holy more accessible and communicable, it can serve to promote our immediate experience of the Holy.

UNITY

We have found that we experience a sacred transcendent reality which we call the Holy, and that our experience happens most intimately in and through love. In love, we also experience a certain unity with the Other, within self, and with the world.

I experience a deep and intimate unity with the human and holy Other. I feel close to, in harmony with, and one with the Other. In this holy communion I lose myself and yet I feel most uniquely myself. Indeed it is true that I become myself by giving myself. I discover that it is good and enjoyable to be in this holy presence.

I also experience unity within my being, for when I encounter the Holy the various parts of myself seem to unify into a harmonious whole. I gain a sense of integrity—a wholeness permeated with holiness. I begin to feel congruent with my experience, and although I may be at odds with myself in my everyday life, I now feel familiar with myself. I find the courage to admit what and who I am.

Furthermore, I experience the harmony and unity of the pre-reflective lived world—the world that precedes the reflective and analytic approach of the ego. My world of the Holy is a world to be with, not a world to be against. Although I may experience tension, my tension is of joy, fascination, excitement, respect, and mystery. My healthy tension is a result of creative growth into the human and holy Other, not a result of unhealthy problems. I am inclined to be in harmony with my pain because I realize that my suffering is in service of life-emergence. Even though I tremble, I rejoice in my trembling.

My unity in the holy experience helps me to experience reality in its unity. I feel at home with life. I see the untouched whole—the integer—of reality and I experience myself as being part of this integer. I do not feel at odds with reality, but my total being is experienced as being one with the whole of reality. I gladly admit that I am a disciple who is called to celebrate and to dwell on the earth.

CONSEQUENT POSITIVE CHANGES

My holy experiences do not remain in a vacuum, but they promote a number of attitudinal and behavioral changes in my life. All the changes that emerge directly or indirectly from my holy experiences are positive, for they are rooted in love—the wellspring of holiness and healthiness. Even crisis, confusion, and disintegration can be positive when they are part of a growth process.

My holy experiences influence all of my experiences. My spiritual experiences are more inclined to take on a holy aspect, and my ego and body modes of behavior may become less impersonal and more influenced by my holy disposition. For example, my work begins to incorporate a transcendent and holy meaning, and my body mode of existence becomes more spontaneous, alive, and emergent. My holy experiences encourage me to embrace the world so that even my day-to-day living takes on a spirit of holiness.

The mark of a holy person is love for reality, including people and the Holy. Holy persons are persons of love. Their holy love orientation motivates them to be available to others and to promote their welfare. We will show in our discussion of "lovism" in Chapter 4 that holy love is neither masochistic or sadistic, but such love is an authentic concern for fostering community—the unity of self-God-other.

Since love is the highest value in my hierarchy of values, it centralizes and influences all my other values. All other activities are second in priority to love for and from the human and holy Other. Consequently, I realize the importance of taking time out for the Holy to spend time with God. I am careful not to displace God with work or another activity so that I find myself so busy that life passes me by. Thus, I structure my life so that I can encounter the human and holy Other both in solitude and with others.

If I am a holy person, people tend to feel at home with me. They know that a loving person can be trusted and will listen. My love is offered in terms of an invitation, not in terms of a forceful demand, and I promote peace and understanding. Through my holy encounters I grow in the understanding of how the world can and should function. I am prone to see the potential of people rather than just their present facticity. I see not only what a person is but also what a person can be. Because of my love, I accept, affirm, and appreciate others in their uniqueness and I respect them as such. I do not intrude on their privacy, but I take a respectful distance toward them. I give them room to be.

I also manifest and am a witness to all those qualities which are congruent with a love orientation: peace, wisdom, understanding, acceptance, respect, compassion, availability, affirmation, integrity, pride, humility, etc. Although I never fully realize these virtues, I strive for and realize them throughout life. My holy transcendence also enables me to see life in terms of unity and integration, not separation and disintegration. Thus, I am unlikely to be seduced by aspects of reality—parts that are identified with the whole, but as a holy person I am more inclined to keep myself in perspective, and a respect for reality comes spontaneously. Being in touch with my self and the Other, I tend to look for the deeper and longer lasting values in others and I tend to see through the social masks to the inner self of others. Because of my taking a distance from immature, unhealthy, and phony situations, I may seem distant at times. In fact, holy persons are distant from the seduction of everyday and work life because they are more apt to see beyond these situations. On the other hand, holy persons are the most compassionate of people in that they enter into our humanity. They have the ability to suffer with (and to celebrate with) others.

In being holy, I am also a witness to the Holy in my culture. My holy witness is basically accomplished in my day-to-day living, so that my very lifestyle reveals the Holy in my life. My life becomes a constant and spontaneous manifestation of the Holy. My witness is not accomplished fundamentally by formal education, but through a lived presence that is experienced pre-reflectively by others. I realize that the Holy must manifest itself in the culture, that the sacred is decidedly profane, and that the Holy is for the culture. I take on a responsibility to and for the culture because I know that a culture that tends to live only for the present and that lacks a holy and transcendent perspective becomes a fragmented and shallow culture. When a culture denies the Holy, it is committing cultural suicide. Unfortunately, contemporary Western culture tends to repress or to dissociate the Holy from the current of life and tends to pressure people to displace the Holy in favor of a life centered around technology and possessions. Our paramount point is that people are needed more than ever to stand up for the Holy in our technocratic-secularistic culture. Without holy people the culture will dissipate into a narcissistic theism. The holy person is the vanguard and guardian of the Holy.

Another consequence of my holy experiences is that I manifest a certain directedness in life. I seem to know where I am going. My life has meaning in the presence of the human and holy Other; life makes sense. I know that life without the Holy becomes meaningless, and this sense gives me a solidarity. Holy persons are usually reliable and dependable because they have a bearing and a consistency in life. Along with holy directedness, I gain long-range values. I have a good sense of history and of the future, and my presence becomes a dialogue of the past and future. Through my spiritual experience of the human and holy Other, my life becomes one of commitment and lasting values. Temporary satisfactions do not become the center of my life, but my life does take on a sense of comprehensive universality. Because I am always beyond myself, my most basic and influential values tend to go beyond themselves.

As a holy person I also become a good person, for I try to promote the common welfare of others and self. I am oriented toward promoting life-emergence, and I know that the greatest way to promote goodness is to love. However, my love is not fantasy love, because, depending upon my degree of psychological health, I implement my love and thereby change the world. Through my love I do good to the world and consequently I live a morally good life. My morality is not a submission to a system of abstract rules, but the spirit of the rules does permeate my life. Although evil does not fit in my holy life, I admit that my potential for evil is always present.

Furthermore, I become a person of faith and hope. My most important values are accepted mainly in faith, and my holy motivation is rooted in faith. In faith I accept the mystery of my own existence, and in hope I wait in ready expectation for its emergence. Being hopeful, I realize that if certain conditions are set, life or people will more likely emerge. Since I live in faith and hope, I am not bound by the clear and distinct—by what can only be communicated objectively. I transcend the seduction of scientism. Life in faith and hope becomes less complicated and takes on an underlying simplicity. I promote a style of play and simplicity in my dialogue with life. Faith and hope in life is no longer a trite statement, but it becomes a lived axiom.

My faith, hope, and love lead to trust. I feel at home in the world. I have less of a need to defend myself because I trust that the holy life in love makes sense. My trust is not an unhealthy dependency wherein I petition the Holy to do things that are my responsibility, but my trust emerges from an affirmation of the sense in the Holy and of its future emergence. For instance, I can begin to accept and understand death as a painful but integral part of life that gives my existence a deeper meaning. My trust in the Holy also makes me less dependent on things outside my personal realm, for I invest my life in love rather than in a peripheral accumulation of possessions. Finally, trust in God enables me to let go of that which I cannot control and place my will and life in holy care.

We have already said that a holy person is charismatic. My charisma means that I inspire others toward looking in different directions and that I evoke respect and listening in others. My charisma is an appeal to others in love to be themselves. My charisma, however, is never forced on others. Its import lies in the fact that it is a dynamic invitation. My sensitivity to others in love makes others more accepting of me and says to others that it is good and acceptable to be yourself. My companions feel that I want their good; they feel that I am on their side and that I am willing to be for them. Thus, a holy person says yes to the wholeness and holiness of self emergence.

My sincerity is not a maudlin view of the world, but it is simply an honestly proud and humble stand toward the world. I grow in honesty in relation to my holiness. I am proud in that I affirm the privilege and joy of leading a holy life, and I am humble in that I am grateful for the gift of the Holy. My pride helps me to affirm reality, and my humility helps me to listen to reality and be less inclined to impose myself on others. My pride and humility help me to have the courage and respect needed for a healthy and holy existence.

In my holiness, I am always going beyond to new horizons and becoming dynamic in my lifestyle. This does not mean that I am explicitly dynamic in that I am outspoken or draw crowds, though some people do have the temperament or ability for this type of behavior. Even though I may be quiet, I am dynamic in that I am constantly emerging and experiencing reality. Living a spirited life, I tend to lack defensiveness and to promote a spontaneity that impresses people. My spontaneous and charismatic love enables people to say that I am a holy person.

Finally, in and through my love with the human and holy Other I discover salvific meaning in my life. I find and live the ground of my being—love for and from the Holy. I escape the normal and mad life of maintenance and meaninglessness and I refuse to fulfill myself fundamentally with anything but the Holy. I discover that life in love makes saving sense.

CONCLUSIONS

Finally, let us focus on our holy experience as an existential and experiential reality. We have proposed that our relation to the Holy is an existential reality. We find ourselves structurally and dynamically related to the human and holy Other. A yes to the Holy is a yes to self, and a yes to self is a yes to the Holy. Thus, if we opt to be open in love to the manifestation of the human and holy Other, we own up to what we are—orientated to the Other.

An increasing tendency exists to analyze God as a projection of self. The main theme of this approach is that we create a supernatural being to protect ourselves from our limited and precarious existence. Strict Freudian believers see God as an illusion that fulfills our urgent wishes of humankind. They analyze our need for protection against helplessness and weakness, proposing that we project a divine father figure in order to gain security.

Many contemporaries consider the traditional conceptions of God in terms of its being a mythology or an anthropomorphic wish projection. Proponents of this "projection approach" say that the creation of the Holy helped us to understand our ignorance and to control our helplessness. This group proposes that the Holy served as a useful symbol of our striving for perfection or as a meaningful explanation of the cosmos. Because of the advent of scientific and evolutionary views, modern religion should be an open and scientific search for the questions and answers of humankind and the universe. The *tremendum* should be met not with mythological gods but with a scientific testing of hypotheses about the unknown.

All these people in some way affirm the reality of an experience called holy, sacred, or religious. They focus, however, on the etiology of religion and/or the religious experience. Basically, they maintain that the religious experience excludes a sacred reality outside us so that the Holy is totally a function of people or society.

These and other criticisms of the religious experience should not be dismissed, for they contain much truth. They are excellent descriptions of forms of inauthentic religion or of modes of our displacement of the Holy. The fundamental error of this approach is that it fails to account for the factors and dynamics of spiritual experiences in general and the constituents of sacredness, transcendence, charisma, love, and consequent positive changes in particular. For instance, these persons do not admit the interpersonal or dialectical dynamic in their analyses of the holy experience, nor do they differentiate the consequences of the authentic holy experiences from those of the inauthentic. Since projection theory only incorporates the constructs of body and ego or similar and related constructs, these theorists futilely try to explain spiritual experiences in terms of the body (id, primary processes, etc.) and ego (secondary processes, social self, etc.). Consequently, reality is perverted in favor of theory instead of changing the theory to incorporate the experience. Truth, however, is discovered in experience, not in theory.

3   Our Experience of No-thingness

I AM CONVINCED that certain kinds of suffering are not only common but also crucial and necessary experiences for a healthy and holy life. In fact, a paramount theme of this book is that the pain of self-encounter—"no-thingness"—is the prelude for encountering the human and holy Other. We will first focus on the common signs, symptoms, dynamics, and significance of all experiences of no-thingness and will follow this general analysis with a concrete discussion of the stages of no-thingness.

THE GENERAL EXPERIENCE OF NO-THINGNESS

We see that we never live in a vacuum, but that we are always involved in the world and with others. Although I usually take reality for granted, or experience it more or less intimately at other times, the meaning of my world and others changes. Instead of being in direct or indifferent relation to them, my world and others become more present in their absence. The "things" that are outside but related to me take second priority to me. Emphasis is on me rather than on what is outside me. The experience of no-thingness occurs when the world and others recede into the background of my world, leaving me with myself in the foreground. No-thingness is the gift of self-confrontation. I come face to face with myself. The core of my existence is thrown into focus, and I am called to take stock of myself.

In no-thingness I am lonely. I feel the presence of the Other in absence. To a certain degree, the world becomes a stranger to me. Yet, I yearn for the Other. I miss people and want to be with them. My lonely experience is more or less intense in that I am in a state of tension between a striving to be with others and an inability to fulfill my desire. Consequently, I am frustrated. What I want I cannot get. Since my inability to be with another person does not depend on the physical presence of people but on their psychological absence, I may be lonely in the physical presence of others.

I may experience healthy loneliness in being sick or when I am faced with the sickness or death of a loved one. The demands of illness, for instance, promote a withdrawal from God and others and at the same time a yearning for them. The paradoxical bind is that it is difficult to be sick alone or with others because sickness simultaneously calls out to the Other for care, physical and psychological, and to be left alone. Consequently, illness without care by the Other or without privacy becomes an illness in itself. This type of healthy loneliness is temporary at least in its acute phases and is realistic in respect to its cause.

The loneliness of no-thingness permeates my existence. My yearning for the human and holy Other is unsatisfied, for although the Other is familiar to me, I cannot get close to the Other. I may search in futility for God, but God remains beyond my reach. Even though I may be deeply in love, my beloved, in my acute phases of no-thingness, becomes more present in her absence. Although physically present, the Other is not psychologically close to me while I am in the throes of no-thingness. My cry for the Other often goes unheard except by myself. My loneliness may envelope me to such a degree that I too may become inaccessible to the Other. It may be comforting to know that the holy Other is there for me, but remains "there" because I do not really experience God as being with me.

However, because I can progressively grow in a deeper sensitivity to self, God, and others through the stages of no-thingness, my pain prepares me for the joy of being with others. Ultimately, therefore, my lonely experience in no-thingness is oriented toward the Other. Through self-confrontation I am made more available to the Other, and through yearning for the Other I learn to appreciate and care for the Other. Thus, the loneliness of no-thingness is healthy when it is oriented toward growth in love of self, others, and God—us.

Analogously, a man who is physically separated from his beloved misses and yearns for her, so that his absence can serve as an opportunity to rekindle and deepen his love. However, his yearning in nothingness is even more basic than this separation, for it occurs within him regardless of his environmental situation. In a very real sense, our yearning for the Other in no-thingness keeps us honest and promotes growth by pressuring us to renew our love for the Other. We can see and care for the Other in a new and deeper way. Love—the highest order—emerges from the quasi chaos of no-thingness.

On the other hand, unhealthy loneliness is based on a yearning that is oriented primarily toward one's own satisfaction—not love for the Other. Although decidedly human, we unconsciously exploit the Other. We want to use the Other to satisfy our needs. We are willing to give, but only in order to receive. Our needs frequently center around dependency, estrangement, or existential frustration—that is, a lack of fundamental meaning in life. We are usually afraid to expose and openly give ourselves to the Other, for we are compelled to see the Other in terms of selfish gratification. The Other is a symbolic breast from which we must suckle for life. Since we are unable to give ourselves unconditionally, our loneliness yearning can never be satisfied and our intrapersonal relations usually remain temporary or primarily matters of fantasy.

In contrast to loneliness, I can be alone wherein I am physically by myself. I have more control over my experiences of aloneness than over those of loneliness. I can will to be alone; I cannot will to be lonely. When I am alone I can be psychologically with people, that is, not lonely. Aloneness can also be thrust upon me against my will. Nevertheless, I can transcend my situation by being very much alone and yet not lonely. On the other hand, aloneness increases the possibility of being lonely by decreasing defenses against loneliness. The key factor in healthy or unhealthy aloneness is whether I can opt to be open to and for reality. Aloneness is unhealthy when I choose to be alone because I am afraid to face myself and the Other. Whereas, healthy aloneness is ultimately in service of life-emergence.

Solitude occurs when I choose to be alone for healthy reasons such as self-exploration, meditation, recollection, study, enjoyment, thinking, listening, and just "being." One of the highest acts of solitude is to do no-thing. Here I can choose to be alone in order to discover and encounter myself in no-thingness. In my solitude there are fewer things to distract me from my no-thingness. Solitude is always healthy, because it means creative discovery and becoming. A healthy life demands that I periodically take time out to be alone in solitude—whether this be in things or in no-thing.

Finally, withdrawal can be healthy or unhealthy. Healthy withdrawal can be physical and is aloneness and possibly solitude. I can withdraw from others to be with myself in no-thingness.

Withdrawal can also be psychological, as when I withdraw from a group interaction and people say that I am "out of it." Being out of it may be a form of healthy withdrawal in that it is sometimes necessary to protect myself from the demands of a situation. When I am being pressured unjustly by others I must withdraw in order to maintain my sanity. I must also take periodic and creative retreats from the world in order to recreate, and one of the highest forms of retreat is to withdraw into no-thingness. If I never withdraw to find myself, I will eventually lose myself.

Withdrawal is unhealthy usually when there is a refusal or inability to face the fear of being hurt. A psychotic person, for example, often withdraws because he is afraid of being destroyed or of being hurt by another. The paradox is that the psychotic's admirable attempt to save himself via withdrawal results in a chronic case of self-destruction. Normal people also withdraw for unhealthy reasons when they are afraid to face unpleasant and unacceptable aspects of themselves or of others. This does not mean that we must expose ourselves to being hurt, but we ought to admit what is going on, and then, if necessary, withdraw in a healthy way. In order to say yes or no in a healthy way I must first admit what is going on, for only when I know what is happening can I do something about it. The most unhealthy form of withdrawal occurs when I withdraw from myself. Since I refuse to accept the gift of no-thingness, I become out of touch with myself. Being alienated, I cannot authentically communicate with the Other, for my self withdrawal precludes encounter with the Other. Thus, unhealthy withdrawal is fundamental negation in contrast to the basic affirmation of healthy withdrawal.

We can see that in no-thingness I am thrown back on myself; my existence is "depressed." I am often depressed because I feel that I may lose the ground for my existence. I feel lost in my no—thingness. I also lose the familiar sense of the things around me.

The Other is different, values change, and my past world is suddenly outdated. I am distant from the world of things and I am "pressed in" on myself. My once-familiar world is foreign, leaving me with nothing to grasp.

Being depressed, I may also experience guilt and frustration. I may feel that I have not lived up to my past expectations, that I am unworthy for that world out there, or that I am to blame for the emptiness of my world. Guilt may impinge upon my life—a guilt which says that I am responsible for my painful lot. My existence, being turned in on itself, results in a basic frustration. The Other—for whom my existence is destined—is beyond my grasp. No—thing is closer to me than others. My striving to make sense out of things makes me frustrated, and realizing that no—thing makes the most sense may leave me immersed in frustra-tion.

I also experience existential anxiety and dread in no—thingness. My anxiety is a painful experience resulting from a crucial change that seems to have no purpose. I feel the ground of my life being undermined and thrown into a bottomless pit. My anchorage found in things gives way, and I am left in the middle of no—thing. There is no-thing to cope with and seemingly no-where to go. I also dread losing myself in no-thingness. I feel primordially uneasy, and the primitive feeling of being permanently lost makes me feel helpless in the face of my no-thingness. To be caught in the vortex of no-thingness is the thing I most dread. However, my dread calls me back to the roots of my existence. In dread I question the ground of my existence and I wonder about the possibility of any behavior whatsoever.

These experiences are often painful but necessary and healthy for deeper growth into life, because loneliness, solitude, withdrawal, depression, emptiness, guilt, frustration, anxiety, and dread in no-thingness lead to self-expression for life. Although I stand in anxiety on the precarious ground of no-thingness, my anxious pain in no-thingness prepares me to be with and for the Other. In no-thingness I discover transcendent meaning and the freedom to dwell in and to enjoy the world. Paradoxically, my suffering enables me to say yes to life.

Thus, the apparent nonsense and the experienced pain of no-thingness lead to sense and to a deeper celebration of life. The gift of no-thingness means that I have the opportunity to face and own up to myself. For instance, I can learn to admit my limits. No longer do I live in the magical world of childhood where I can do and be anything I wish; fantasy will no longer satisfy the demands of reality. Now I painfully realize that every decision is a decided limitation, and I am forced to make decisions. It hurts to learn limits, but authentic realizations are possible only with an affirmation of limits.

Furthermore, living the experience of no-thingness promotes a healthy sensitivity. I learn to face and to be in touch with myself; and the more I am in tune with myself, the greater the probability that I can be in tune with others. I discover that when I learn to express myself to myself I will be more ready to express myself to others. My self-expression becomes an art, much of which is acquired in the experience of no-thingness. My self articulation also becomes a wellspring of creativity, and new insights and modes of expression emerge in my loneliness. My new views are not just oriented toward the world of the arts, but more fundamentally my insights are new sights into life. I find that becoming myself is the most important and fundamental form of creativity and that it serves as the ground for all other forms of creativity.

In no-thingness I realize that no one can give me freedom or make me healthy. I discover that I must earn my authenticity by learning and living the meaning of authentic dependency, independency, and interdependency. I admit that these projects are my responsibility and that although others influence and help me, no one except me can live my life.

The crisis in no-thingness also leads me to a reevaluation of my standards. I now ask the questions: What is truth for me? How can I live my standards? How can I modify my standards so that they are in harmony with my experience? How can I make values mine without rejecting the past and those who gave me my values? This crisis is a crisis of my life—my identity in life. The fundamental questions emerge: Who am I? What am I? Where am I going? Whence do I come? Why should I live? What do I want my heritage to be? What is my life project?

I am also presented with the opportunity to admit what I am, so that I can come to a painfully exciting and new stand toward myself. I may discover that I am hateful toward my loved ones, that I consider myself inadequate, that I have little respect for myself, that I see myself as one with little value, and that I am unworthy of love and therefore unworthy of loving. In the same experience I may uncover the true love I have for myself and for others, the possibilities and talents that I never realized, true respect toward myself, and myself as a person of value and uniqueness, a person who is worthy of love and of loving.

Furthermore, my experience of no–thingness often offers me the possibility to change my life orientations. I may see in new ways or affirm past options in a new light. Being thrust into a crisis of self-identity, I may discover new commitment in life or may reaffirm past commitment. New self-discoveries, experiences, insights, possibilities, and limits are confronted. In certain instances I may even come close to despair, but from these depths I may rise to a greater level of personal integration. For example, a student may have to take a retreat from her life situation in order to find herself for a creative return. Depending upon their personal history, some persons may even experience a psychotic disintegration that could lead to a creative reintegration. It is not rare for people to become healthier from a psychotic experience when they accept, integrate, and learn from their psychotic experience instead of trying to forget and return to their previous state of mad maintenance.

After I have lived through my no–thingness, I also have the opportunity to experience the Holy. Although my holy experience presupposes and depends on my experience of no–thingness, it is not a guarantee of an overt holy experience, but is only a preparation for the Holy. If I live through and own up to myself in no–thingness and if I remain available to the Holy, I will probably experience the Holy. However, my holy encounters may remain implicit for decades or for a lifetime even though my love of other people is explicit.

In short, the crisis of no–thingness is important because we experience a self-confrontation that is a necessary prelude for the experience of the Other. When we discover ourselves in the crisis of no–thingness, we become ready to present ourselves to the human and holy Other. Our no–thingness leads us to being with reality. We are freed to experience love of the Other, wonder in being, and aesthetic joy in beauty.

Now, let us make some general observations about the dynamics and development of no–thingness. We emphasize that the experience of no–thingness and the experience of things are dialectically related. The more I find and become myself in no–thingness, the more available I am to and for reality. On the other hand, my experiences of things, especially other persons, have a great influence on my experience of no–thingness; my experiences of the Other—before, during, and after my experiences of no–thingness—will partially determine how open I am to my no–thingness. For instance, if people around me give me concerned support in my no–thingness, my chances of living my no–thingness are much greater than if I were made to feel guilty about or encouraged to repress my no–thingness. Thus, my encounters with things presuppose my experiences in no–thingness, and my experiences of no–thingness presuppose my encounters with things.

Although I constantly live in the shadow of no–thingness, it may be brought to the foreground in several ways. A direct experience of no–thingness can occur at any time, but the most common and fundamental way is to experience it at certain stages in life. All the stages of no–thingness are basically the same, although they also differ accidentally but importantly according to the particular stage of development. These developmental crises are very important because they tend to keep me honest. I am confronted with myself in no–thingness, and my decision to accept or reject the experience will determine my future growth. The fruitfulness of my experience depends partially on my preceding life history and experiences of no–thingness, along with such factors as my immediate environment, culture, intrapersonal relationships, and values.

Furthermore, certain situations may evoke the implicit presence of no-thingness to become explicit or they may rekindle a repressed experience of nothingness. For instance, a national catastrophe, a personal crisis, or psychotherapy may promote a self-confrontation in no-thingness that is outside or in addition to the developmental crisis. It is also possible for a disciplined person to opt for some degree of no-thingness. Although this person does not willfully control his no-thingness, he can opt to promote and to be available to a self-confrontation in no-thingness.

From a theoretical perspective, we can see that the word "thing" has a special meaning in describing the experience of no-thingness. When used in everyday parlance, this word usually refers to an inanimate object; but when it is used in reference to no-thingness, "thing" refers to that which is outside but related to me. Things take on a vital meaning by referring to the worlds of culture, inanimate and animate objects, nature, people, and the Holy. Metaphorically, things refer to those situations and activities which are primarily "outside my skin." In no-thingness I am concerned with those experiences happening "within my skin" and primarily with those related or oriented to my spirit.

We can also discern that in my experience of no-thingness my body and ego modes of existence also recede into the background, and (with the exception of the negative stage) I am left with no-thing except my spirit. I become existentially introspective and spontaneously look within myself especially in my more acute moments. My body and ego, however, do not cease their functioning, for I am still very much in the world in these modes of existence. Although the accent is on my spirit, no-thingness involves my whole being, so that my body and ego are introspected basically in the light of the spirit. For instance, I may "look at" my intelligence or body in terms of its limitations, possibilities, uniqueness, or value. Our crucial point is that the spirit takes on the most significance and attention because the experience calls attention to the spiritual.

Since no-thingness is primarily, although not exclusively, a spiritual experience, the experience is beyond rational thought and decision; no-thingness does not lend itself to lineal and discursive approaches. In a certain sense I go out of my ego mind in the experience of no-thingness. Being a spiritual experience, the experience of no-thingness is in the realms of mystery and paradox. Although my body feels intensely the no-thingness and my ego reflects on it, the accent is on my spirit—the most intimate expression of my being.

In the following sections I propose that we go through certain stages of holiness and that ideally they are correlated with his stages of nothingness. I relate each degree of holiness to a stage of no-thingness. Although most people experience the crisis within or near the age range, the ranges are not absolute.

NO-THINGNESS IN EARLY ADOLESCENCE

The initial encounter with no-thingness is a negative experience of no-thingness, which usually occurs in early adolescence, somewhere in the age range of thirteen to sixteen. The experience does not coincide exactly with prepuberty and puberty, although its onset may emerge during or at the end of puberty. Girls often experience it a little sooner than boys. The "Catcher in the Rye," Holden Caulfield, or the notorious sophomore in high school are examples of people in this negative stage of no-thingness.

Although as a young adolescent I am not constantly and directly experiencing my no—thingness, I do have times of direct confrontation. Here I am bored; I have no—thing to do or be, and although I have boundless energy, I am tired. My behavior seems to be aimless and nonintegrated. It is. No—things appeal to me. I am sick and tired of life, even though I have scarcely lived it. No one understands. I feel alone. No-body and no—thing make sense to me. My world is a cosmos of non-sense.

Although I periodically experience the acute phases of no—thingness, an orientation of no—thingness usually permeates my behavior. Like Holden Caulfield, I suspect almost everyone— "the whole damn world is phony." I sharply see the imperfections and mistakes of elders especially those in authority, such as parents and teachers—and I criticize them with ruthless discernment, often to my elders' embarrassment. Parents are often at their wits' end to know what to do with this new edition of son or daughter. The object-poles of the ego and the body, such as work, science, structure, and feelings, recede into the background and make little sense. I take keen delight in criticizing or breaking the rules; obedience is an ambivalent burden. Structure is a painful reminder of my no—thingness. I want no part of it.

The distinguishing feature of this stage is that I am left explicitly with no—thingness—not even the spirit. However, I experience my spirit in its absence; I feel a lack of my spiritual self. Thus, my experience becomes a decidedly negative experience insofar as it is a pre-spiritual confrontation, for my spiritual self has not yet overtly emerged.

This experience is not absolutely negative, however, because it involves a new stand toward my own being, others, and the world, and it also leads to the first direct experience of the spiritual self. Later, several months or years, some will emerge as spirit, and for the first time they will have a direct spiritual experience.

Out of the experience of negative no-thingness, adolescents emerge as a spiritual presence to reality. For the first time, they directly actualize and express their spiritual self. Again, I appear to change suddenly, and my parents' patience—for time to cure—has paid. No longer am I bored or living in non-sense. Just the opposite, I am enchanted and romantically in love with everything. Suddenly I experience the world in an entirely new way. For the first time, I may begin to write poetry or to see life from a philosophical perspective. I still criticize, although not from a sense of boredom but from a sense of romantic idealism. Before, nothing was possible, now everything is possible. My pessimism changes to optimism. Although the realities of the concrete situation usually limit my idealism and my future is uncertain, basic enthusiasm persists.

Realities take on an added dimension, for they are now stimuli for romanticism, poetry, or wonder. Teachers are no longer an object of criticism, but they may become a source of inspiration. Teenagers begin to think of life commitment, which is a new experience for them. "Where am I going?" becomes a lived question from within, not an irritating question asked by someone else from without.

These emergent adolescents experience love in a new way, for love now incorporates responsibility, respect, and commitment. Love is no longer only for the moment. Love points to long-range plans. Although love tends to be romantic and idealistic, it is also experienced in terms of life projects; I begin to think in terms of life commitment in regard to love and vocation. Since my love now incorporates the sacred, I experience the Other more deeply. In fact, I begin to feel a kinship with humankind. Furthermore, I encounter the Holy in solitude, so that moments of loneliness begin to make new sense to me. I may, in fact, begin to cultivate such situations.

An explicit experience of the human and holy Other also emerges from no-thingness. In the past young adolescents enjoyed an implicit presence to the Holy. Now they are presented with the opportunity for more direct holy encounters. Although their holy experience is not of the same intensity and quality as the mature and holy adult's, their experience does incorporate all the constituents necessary for a holy experience. In mid-adolescence, I begin to experience a numinous and paradoxical transcendence embedded in a sacred mystery. I also begin to experience a new sense of dependency and indebtedness; and love, faith, and doubt become very real issues. In short, my encounter with the Other offers new experiences that I must integrate. I am initiated into a life in the presence of the Holy, and the consequent positive changes from holy experiences begin to emerge. I am a novice in spirituality.

Adolescents also start to personalize the rules of life. I begin to see new possibilities in structures. Structures begin to become opportunities for transcendence and freedom, not shackles as in the recent past. Transcendence gives me the freedom to increase my field of possibilities; and although these possibilities are initially played with in fantasy, they are nevertheless real. Morality, for instance, has new meaning for me; I begin to respect and be genuinely concerned for the Other. My standards for goodness go beyond the here-and-now and include the future. However, at times I may reflect and try to make explicit sense out of the holy experiences. Sometimes adolescents will "think" very much about their new experiences, not so much in terms of the Holy but in terms of responsibility, and this ultra-concern for responsibility may take the form of temporary scrupulosity. Adolescents, especially ones with compulsive tendencies, may become obsessively concerned about the morality of their behavior. This moralistic behavior is usually temporary and can serve as a means of growth by leading them to a true meaning of morality.

Parents and teachers are especially frustrated by this developmental stage, particularly in its negative phase. They too often try with good intentions to get rid of the negativity. They see this experience as a problem to be solved rather than a necessary experience to be understood and affirmed. It must be realized and accepted that the particular kind of negativity and ambiguity of this stage is painful but healthy. Nevertheless, adolescents must live through this stage in order to develop. If the future is kept in perspective, their negativity will make more sense. However, if the parents try to force them to become mature before their time, these adolescents will only suffer needlessly and risk unhealthy frustrations in development. Parents can help by understanding and accepting their children's experience and give them a realistic amount of freedom to grow. They can be available when their teenagers may call on them, and above all they can give them the courage through love to accept and live their experience in a meaningful and fruitful way.

This experience of no-thingness is the easiest of all the stages to live through because there is less danger of rejection, distortion, fixation, and pathological decisions. The adolescent's resiliency and ignorance decrease the possibility of pathological coping mechanisms. Furthermore, there are no direct spiritual experiences to make sense out of and to integrate such as in the later stages of no–thingness. The adolescent's youth is often a saving grace.

On the other hand, young adolescents may undergo unhealthy experiences of no–thingness. Because of a pathological personality, a person may never reach the stage of development of no–thingness. Or, a person whose basic needs, such as hunger, sleep, security, and love, have been seriously unsatisfied may not be sufficiently mature to experience no–thingness. An adolescent may also become threatened by the experience and regress to an earlier level of development or become fixated in no–thingness for a long period of time. An example of such a person is the individual who is in his third decade of life and is still aimlessly roaming the earth in a negative no–thingness. The fixation, however, will usually develop into a pathological existence if not resolved in a healthy way, for the life demands of this person cannot be adequately integrated.

Young adolescents find themselves out of no–thingness. Functions of spirit begin to emerge, and they have their first overt spiritual experiences. Although they are neophytes, they do begin the life projects of mature love, responsibility, commitment, morality, freedom, etc., including the spiritual experiences of the human and holy Other.

NO–THINGNESS IN LATE ADOLESCENCE

Our next stage of no–thingness occurs after the first direct experience of the spiritual self, usually in the late teens and/or early twenties. The outstanding feature of this stage is that it offers the first positive experience of no–thingness. The dynamics once again involve the recession of things, especially the object-poles of the body and ego; but this time we have the first true crisis of spiritual identity. The world and others are distant in favor of the most vivid reality—our spirit.

In college, many students experience no—thingness most acutely in their sophomore year. The experiences of teachers and students along with empirical studies have shown that the sophomore year is significantly different from other college years. The lonely, withdrawn, bored, and angry sophomore is notorious. The apparently alive freshman may seem to turn suddenly into a confused sophomore whose value system has changed radically.

Sophomores confuse not only themselves but also others. They are nowhere, have difficulty thinking of anything, and cannot get close to anyone. Intrapersonal crisis is dominant, and coming close to or being in despair is not infrequent. The sophomore is in school, but more fundamentally in no—thingness. This sophomore moratorium is a necessary prelude to a mature life. As a student once said: "One must become disenchanted with life before she can become enchanted with life."

The adolescent's recent idealism is replaced by a sharp self-criticism. Spiritual values, which were played with, are now considered from a different perspective. I see my others' limits, and ideals seem unattainable. I recognize my needs for meaning and love in life and wonder if they will ever be satisfied. Commitment becomes very clear, but commitment to what and how? I ask myself if I will ever become a mature adult. I am confused as to who I am, my future is threatening and foreign, and my past is a source of painful realizations.

The present situation becomes meaningless and empty; things outside myself can no longer fulfill me. I begin to look at myself differently and start to reevaluate my standards, which I used to take for granted. What is truth for me becomes a very serious question. I can no longer habitually follow a system of shoulds that comes from without; I strive to live according to fundamental oughts that come from within. Some questions emerge: What are obedience, love, respect, maturity, responsibility, and freedom? The classical questions emerge: Who am I? Where am I going? Whence do I come? Why am I? The accepted rules of the past are permeated with "why?" Everything is brought into question in no-thingness.

Since I discern my inherited "shoulds," I usually become more or less angry at my past—especially with my parents. I see the limits and imperfections of these shoulds and I realize what I did not receive and perhaps should have received from my parents. A common danger is that I become fixated in this stage and refuse to grow until I have received what I think I have the right to receive.

It may be frightening for me to realize that freedom and autonomy must develop primarily from within oneself and are not acquired from external agents. Frequently, I look outside myself for the source of freedom, such as parents or the structure of a situation. Many persons in this stage initially go through the process of rebellion toward their superiors and especially their parents. They make their pleas in many forms. "You won't let me be free." "My parents don't bother me—I cut the ties." These and other similar approaches incorporate a dependency in that these late adolescents feel that only the Other (superior) can give them their freedom. "If only this were changed, if I could do this, then I would be free" is a common adolescent experience that must be resolved. In other words, if I constantly criticize or brag of my freedom from my parents, I am probably quite dependent on them. I must learn to admit my dependency to attain true freedom.

Sometimes late adolescents may physically run away from home, deluding themselves that they have run away from their parents. Little do they realize that their parents within them—biologically and psychologically—can never be severed, but can be faced, understood, and integrated into the totality of their personalities. When I personalize the assets and deficits of my parents within myself, I can authentically transcend them.

Responsibility also becomes a paramount issue. In late adolescence, I wonder how I can find the ability to respond to life. I feel inadequate, but nevertheless I vigorously fight my deficiency. Left with myself, I realize that true responsibility rests on me and this is quite different from my past life. It may frighten me to know that in terms of responsibility I may now have to become in some ways a parent to my parents. I must be able to accept and understand my parents in all their positive and negative humanity, and I can no longer see my parents as, or demand that they be, perfect and divine. Nor can I lead a basically dependent and wishful life and be a mature adult. I must give up the ways of his past, but my future ways are uncertain and not yet attainable. My world is distant, and I do not yet know my spiritual self which must live in and guide my future. I am left in a bind, but my bind is temporary.

A common symptom of this stage is doubt. I suddenly doubt most of my values and standards that I took for granted. Religion is usually a prime target of my critical evaluation so that probably for the first time I ask critical questions concerning my religious belief. When I realize the imperfections and errors in my inherited religious system, I may feel that I have been duped into living a phony religious system. I may feel embarrassed and give up all religious practices and beliefs, so that suddenly I am no longer practicing what I recently valued. I may sometimes attack those who profess to live the religious life, behavior that is often an unconscious attempt to make sense out of my own religion. Not all late adolescents confront their religious belief with such intensity, but most, if not all, do seriously question it.

The dangers of unhealthy experiences and resolutions are far greater in this stage than in the preceding one. A common danger is that one's loneliness may become unhealthy. If a person has had past experiences of rejection or hyper-dependency, he or she may become fixated on the absence of the Other. Such persons may feel that life depends on the love of the Other, because their salvation from no-thingness is completely out of their hands. They lose all autonomy and long for the panacea of the Other's affection. The bind is that these people are usually afraid to give themselves fully, for the very experience that they feel will save them, they also feel could destroy them. Therefore, they tend to go from person to person—never giving completely and never letting go completely unless and until the Other becomes too threatening. The greatest danger is that this person will move from loneliness to despair. All hope in finding the Other to fulfill the nothingness is lost. It is not rare, for example, to play with the possibility of suicide.

This experience of no-thingness may be delayed or frustrated for various reasons. For instance, the experience may be delayed because of a life situation which makes it less probable for this crisis to occur. The soldier in combat, the starving person, the immature person, and the mentally ill are a few examples. Why is it difficult to live through the experience and benefit from it? Why does one refuse the gift of no-thingness often in the forms of escapism, displacement, repression, regression, and sublimation?

The experience is painful; to be alone, empty, lonely, and feeling one's limits, hurts. People in the Western culture are usually conditioned to refuse or at best to tolerate pain. Pain is senseless to Western civilization. Living according to this pleasure principle, we find it difficult to accept the fact that we can be liberated through pain, to realize that the road to maturity is fraught with the uncomfortable.

Furthermore, seldom is a person really given support or permission to be alone, because lonely experiences threaten others who may never have faced their own no-thingness. Elders frequently try to divert young people's attention from their nothingness. Although they have sincere intentions, many parents and teachers try to save them from their suffering. They try to seduce late adolescents into activity—study, read, go to a movie, dance, or party, walk, talk, join the service, work, etc.—do anything except no-thing.

Many persons become anxious about their no-thingness, often because they try to escape from their existential loneliness. For instance, I fight a losing battle when I try to deny what I am, a lonely person in no-thingness. I become at odds with myself, never really being at home with myself. I am constantly restless and restive. This anxious and lonely existence will not be resolved until I can face myself in no-thingnessness, and therefore have the possibilities to give and to be with others.

Finally, the experience of no-thingness is contrary to Western cultural values. An overly pragmatic society makes no room for no-thingness—the ultimate sin is to do no-thing. We feel guilty if we cannot justify what we are doing, for the culture measures worth in terms of what we have produced, not what we are. This pragmatic infrastructure of the culture makes it more difficult to

85

cope authentically with the experience of no–thingnessness.

We contend that we have the right to suffer because if our experiences are thwarted, we cannot mature. Irritating behavior, such as doubt and criticism, should be allowed and understood in support of the future emergence of self and other. Opinions and feelings need not be condoned in order to be accepted, for there is room for disagreement if it is based on love and respect. This suffering is part of development and should be allowed to evolve and work itself out. If accepted, the suffering will disappear in time, but if the pain is not accepted, the pain will linger and become worse. Young adults may suffer about their suffering. If their loneliness is not allowed to be, they may also develop inauthentic guilt feelings that tend to exacerbate natural doubt and cover their authentic guilt. Soon they find themselves in a bind—the more doubt, the greater the feeling of guilt and this guilt produces more doubt.

If we are allowed to emerge and are given support in emerging out of our no–thingness, we will come to our second direct experience of spirit and attain young adulthood. This spiritual experience also has its idealistic phase, but it differs from the previous stage in time and quality. We first see and experience the world and self in terms of ideals. The establishment of the elders is particularly under our fire of criticism, and we usually find it difficult to accept the impersonal technology and inhuman policies and structures of society. We are likely to be seduced by fictions such as love in itself is a panacea for the world's problems. We tend to see the world exclusively in terms of spiritual experiences and find it difficult to understand and accept the non-spiritual approach of society. The impersonality of the establishment irritates us, and we consider it an impediment to authentic growth and self-actualization.

In young adulthood I may experience most of the established forms of structure as serious and unjust impediments to freedom, so that I rebel against and resist the imposed rules that are not of my own making. I often dupe myself into thinking that I can live without many of the traditional structures. Later, I will take a more realistic and responsible approach to changing the structures.

In this initial phase, enthusiasm and sacrifice are paramount. Often as a young adult I am willing to make great sacrifices to attain goals and to risk myself in adamant stands. I tend to join groups wherein I get support and wherein my ideals can be partially actualized. Social movements, fraternal organizations, religious and political activities, clubs, gangs, and support groups are a few examples. This ideal stage is basically true as far as it goes, but it errs in its one-sidedness. Nevertheless, it is a healthy phase which we may grow through in various degrees.

Although an exciting and painful time, this initial phase should not last very long. Soon the college protester, the street corner militant, the headstrong celibate, or the enthusiastic married couple settle down. However, if fixation occurs in this phase, they will futilely try to live an adolescent idealism. Such persons do not grow up, because they demand that reality conform to a fictive idealism instead of implementing their ideals in and for reality.

My holy experience may also be influenced by this idealistic phase. I try to live a holy life at the expense of subduing my body and ego modes of existence. Everything is seen as irrelevant as contrasted with love. I try to live holy love constantly, and often those who are loving are accepted. Everything seems so drab except love. Instead of the Holy influencing my daily living, I try to exclude the everyday in favor of being explicitly and constantly holy. Holy, love, encounter, respect, honesty, etc., are the only important words, but I do not realize that body and ego functions are also necessary and healthy in living a holy life. Since I try to keep the Holy constantly in the foreground at the expense of other realities, I may become hypercritical of things and reject the phoniness and imperfections of the world in the cause of holiness.

In this stage, I may have intense holy experiences and may begin to make sense out of them. My sense, however, remains initially and primarily within myself, wherein I wonder about experiences and about how I am going to implement them. I may at first try exaggerated ways, such as changing the world only through good intentions—without time and study. For instance, a person who feels that love will cure mentally ill persons is naive. Although love is the basis of therapeutic treatment, the implementation of love takes years of education. Nevertheless, this idealistic phase is healthy if it is a step in the process of further growth. Since it is common to play with newly discovered holy experiences before being ready to socialize them in realistic ways, such persons should be given time to prepare themselves. If the phases of no–thingness and idealism are lived through in a healthy way, I will begin the process of integrating my spiritual experiences and values within my own being and within the world. I will form a hierarchy of values in which all three levels of existence play an important part, but in which my spiritual is the most important. Although life will center primarily around being an authentic person, the values of having will not be excluded.

I will struggle and succeed with the difficult life project of being a whole person. My body and ego will be inspired by my spirit, and I will grow in becoming a whole and holy person. My enthusiasm (*en theo* = in God) will become more rooted in life.

Since this decade of the twenties calls for life options, such as vocation, commitment, and work, I realize that decisions in my twenties will probably carry me throughout life. In no-thingness I first feel the pressure to decide what I am going to be and do, and the question, How am I going to implement the who that I am? remains unanswered. Will I get married or remain single? Most people are forced to answer the question within several years, and if they wait too long, it may be too late. They are caught in a paradoxical bind. The longer they wait to decide, the fewer the possibilities but the higher the degree of preparation. The sooner they decide, the greater the possibilities but the lesser the degree of readiness. Thus, a person who marries young is more likely to be divorced, and the longer a person remains single, the more difficult it is to get married. Or a person who committed herself too early may become a considerably different person, leaving her in conflict with her past commitment. Unfortunately, most people are not prepared to make vocational or committed decisions, so that their decisions are too often a matter of magical wish fulfillment instead of mature commitment.

In short, the third decade of life is one of crucial introspection and reflection. Reality is thrust upon the young adult. I am confronted with questions that I am usually not prepared to meet. I must decide what to do, who to be, where to go. I can no longer keep these questions within myself; now I must act on them. It is a time when I find myself and how I am going to embody myself in the world. I try to discover the where and how of my niche in the world—how I can be a whole person and leave my mark.

NO–THINGNESSNESS IN ADULTHOOD

The third differentiated stage of no–thingness usually occurs around the age range of thirty to thirty-five. The adult in his thirties is usually very involved in life, and since he has been in his particular style of life for some years, it starts to become crystallized. One wants things to run smoothly without drastic change. Thus, the critical change of nothingness becomes a crucial and painful experience. Once again, we are thrown back on ourselves, and we again experience loneliness, aloneness, depression, self-identity crisis, commitment crisis, etc. This time, however, the experience is different from what it was a decade ago. We experience our spiritual self as a self that has been incarnated and has been a life project, not so much a self that seeks reevaluation and initial commitment. We experience ourselves as more of an adult who has given up the ways of a child and the discoveries of late adolescence. Now we have the opportunity to confront ourselves as adults.

A person in her thirties feels her limits for the first time. Death makes its presence really felt, for death was not really a lived issue in her past life. She may near the halfway mark in her life and therefore may be closer to death than to birth. Although this person does not experience death nearly so intensely as in later life, death does become an issue. In fact, the presence of death makes her life vital. Her being-toward-death makes her anxious for life and encourages her to seek deeper meaning in life.

The fantasy life of the teens and twenties has almost completely vanished, and she finds herself rooted in the world. No longer can she live the ideal romanticism of the teens, at least not in the same way, nor can she play with the unlimited possibilities of life commitment as she did in her twenties. Now she is faced with concrete responsibilities that demand attention. She must live out her commitments and convictions. Psychological time and space are also drastically limited. For instance, life options opened up many possibilities but also precluded others, and experiential time goes by more quickly.

The limitations of the body become apparent. The flesh is weaker than in his recent and youthful past. The axiom, "The spirit is willing but the flesh is weak," takes on new meaning. Now a person experiences his *own* limits—not primarily those of the world. He has to make some embarrassing effort to do things that he once did automatically. Aches and pains appear; personal and financial responsibilities face him; his stability appears to limit his freedom. Social life is curtailed; life is too busy; there is a paucity of fun. These limits of life are experienced acutely and often temporarily out of proportion to his situation.

A woman tends to think more in terms of her personal fulfillment—how satisfied has she been. Although she begins to experience her body limits, she still has just reached the peak of her sexual life. She may begin to play with the possibility of a promiscuous affair, especially if her sexual life has been unsatisfactory. She feels that her ability to seduce a man and the affair may offer the added advantages of escaping from her no-thingness. Soon she will be older and culturally less attractive; so if she is going to fulfill her sexual fantasy life, she had better do it now.

Individuals in this stage of life have a stark realization that they are immersed in life and wonder whether they have made the right decision. If one waits another decade, it is improbable, although not impossible, that he will be able to make a change. If another vocation appeals to him, he had better take the risk at this time. However, this person's life situation makes the crisis difficult. He has settled down and has figured out a way to meet his responsibilities and to make sense in his life. He has acquired some authority or power, and a change would mean an abdication of many of these positions. Change for some people is seen to be an intrusion that upsets a smooth-running life, but others openly face the intrusion of change as an opportunity for further growth. The experience of no-thingness, however, does not mean that a person will necessarily change his life commitment; fundamentally it is an opportunity to explore and be more himself.

Religion becomes a critical issue—in its absence or presence. Being thrown back on herself in nothingness, a woman may seriously question if there is a God. She painfully questions the ground of her existence: Is there a fundamental meaning in life? She critically questions the God of her past; doubt is prevalent, especially with spiritual matters. In no-thingness, she searches for a transcendent meaning—an ultimate concern that can give some ultimate meaning to the life that she has chosen. She asks many questions and often gets no answers. She wonders whether there is such a reality as a God, and she may come to the conclusion that there is not. Yet, she realizes pre-reflectively that the options she makes will have a critical influence on her future life.

Many people find it difficult to live with the apparent nonsense in no-thingness, and a consequent repression of the experience is too common. A person in his thirties is still young and energetic; he has enough ego strength to run away from his spiritual self. Furthermore, a person usually has little time to confront his no-thingness, and he tends to look at his experiences of no-thingness in the same terms as the other experiences of his life— he sees it as a problem. He does not realize that no-thing does not lend itself to problem solving, but that no–thingness must be creatively accepted and eventually made meaningful. No–thingness is an experience for which one must take time. Otherwise, he will find time to be more and more meaningless. He must realize that some things are expedient, but no–thingness is beyond expediency.

If we live through no–thingness, we will come again to new and deeper meanings in the things—the Other and the world. For instance, a husband will see his wife in a new light; he will respect her more deeply. His wife, in turn, will also increase in her love for him. The single person will see new meaning in her vocation; things will light up—they will make deeper sense. A person's life will not be a reluctant going through the motions of living. There will be a reason for being. Here growth into freedom will enable her to transcend the embeddedness of her situation, and she will come to an inner solidarity and centeredness that will give an authentic style to her life. She will come to be the author of her existence, so that people will listen to and follow her basically for what she is—not for the function she has.

The thirties and forties are the decades in which to live and implement commitment. If a true commitment is made, a person will have direction and sense, and his everyday and work activities will be permeated by the radiance of his self. A person's busy life will not be mere business, but his activity will be influenced by a force that makes himself and others whole. Spiritual values of love, openness, commitment, responsibility, transcendence, and so forth will be given a greater degree of reality through deeper articulation and implementation.

A person in his or her thirties also comes to a deeper experience of the Holy. In the crisis of no–thingness, a person's doubts of religion and of God are critical yearnings for the Holy. And concurrently he and she may feel depressed because they feel that they are losing the ground of their existence. No—thingness, however, is an acute indication of the need for holy ground and a sign of a desperate search for ultimate meaning. The groundlessness of no—thingness is a desire for a meaningful ground for existence. We experience more pressure than in the past to face our need for the holy sense, and our development and involvement in the world give us a greater need for holy transcendence.

Our history is an important factor in how we will face our crisis. If a woman has grown from her previous experience, she is more likely to accept her present no—thingness than if she previously rejected herself. A person who escapes no—thingness escapes from herself and the holy ground of her life; she is left with a rootless and meaningless life. However, if a person opts for the Holy, the Holy becomes the core of her existence, so that everything makes sense in the light of the human and the holy Other. Her holy sense does not exclude the world, which was the way of her past idealism, but her holy sense incorporates the world. She knows that body and ego functions are necessary for the expression and implementation of love, and she begins the life project of integrating her love within hertotal being.

She brings her holiness to the world, and her witness to the Holy is actualized realistically to and in the world. People begin to recognize that she is a holy person—a person who behaves within and transcends the system. In a very real sense she takes on a new way of living, one that is centrally motivated by the Holy. Others experience her respect and love, and consequently they know her as a good person. They do not experience her holy orientation as explosive or intrusive, but as serene and strong.

This young person progressively discovers deeper meaning in life—life has purpose. Since the human and holy Other is the highest value in one's hierarchy of values, all values are highly influenced by a holy value. We take the Holy to the world, and our behavior is a radiation of the Holy; everyday living begins to make significant sense in the light of the Holy. Love orientation liberates us for everyday and work behavior, for our groundedness enables us to concentrate fully on work. We do not have to worry needlessly about things, for things make sense. We enjoy recreation. We can play with things. Our holy solidarity and ground also enable us to enjoy sex. It is a way of giving and of being, not merely a means to satisfy ourselves. In short, routine work, play, and love becomes a celebration of the human and holy Other.

Love is our most important mode of behavior. Holiness liberates us to give freely and unconditionally to everyone and particularly to our beloved. We do not dependently seek a return for love because our holy ground supports us. Paradoxically, however, we usually receive love, for we make no demands on the Other. We can afford to love the Other for the Other's sake, and our love appeal invites the Other to love us.

Finally, holy persons are not seduced by the immediacy of things or by the perfection of fantasy. Standing on solid ground, we see more clearly. We may become a mystery to some people, but a mystery that appeals, not threatens. People wonder how we can maintain harmony and perspective, for we do not seem to be caught in the madness of life. People see that life makes sense to us.

NO–THINGNESS IN MIDDLE AGE

The fourth stage of no-thingness, which occurs usually between the ages of forty-five and fifty-five, is often the most intense and painful of all. There are various names for this life phase, such as the involutional period, the crisis of the limits, and the dark night of the soul—all of which refer to the same fundamental experience from a slightly different perspective.

We have gone past the halfway point in life, so we are closer to death than to birth. The reality of death overwhelms us and forces us to take a stand toward the experience of the "not-yet death." Although dying is the strongest limit we face, sensitivity to limits in general permeates our life. Limits and a sense of loss are the key factors in involutional no-thingness. The faces of death and age increase our experience of limits. Limits surround us so much that it is difficult for us to see possibilities because our perception of a limited present and past frustrates our vision of a future.

In involutional no-thingness, everything about life tends to be considered as a failure or at least inadequate. A man (or woman) constantly asks himself if his life has really mattered to anyone, especially to himself. He has raised a family, but how well? Or, when has he loved in his celibacy? He has possessions, but how much? He has worked hard, but for what? He may ask himself: Have I really reached my aspirations? Others have done so much better. What difference does and did my life make? Who really cares for me? Who knows me? Darkness closes in, and this person sees himself as a limitation—as a nothing. He feels that he really does not matter. He feels like a zero, like a no-thing.

He focuses on his limits; his transcendent aspects recede to the background in favor of its rootedness. His spiritual values, often those of ethics, life goals, love, and actualization, are critically questioned. This person says to himself: Time is running out on me. If I am not on the right course, it may soon be too late to find it. I still have time to find myself, but how, where, when? Has my life been true and meaningful, or has it been a meaningless charade? The often trite question, What is the meaning of life? becomes a critically vital question.

Questions concerning the Holy also emerge. Have I worshipped a false god? What is God? What impact does God really have for me? What is my ultimate concern? Have I followed and supported rules that are out of tune with reality? Is the church doing honest and good work? What is my role in the church? Do these realities make sense? Yes and no! Even if I should give them up, what would I have left? No—thing!

A woman's introspective eye also looks critically at her own body and ego. This person is usually sick and tired of thinking. She has found that reason is a valuable means, but for what? Ego processes make little sense without spiritual processes—her ego cannot give her what she is searching for. This person is fed up with being a rational animal. The limitations of her body also demand recognition, for the body is weaker, less resilient and resistant, and more flabby, painful, and tired. Physical fitness becomes a task that is seldom achieved. Furthermore, the physiological changes of the climacteric are usually correlated with her no—thingness and serve to exacerbate basic feelings of being limited, worthless, and inadequate. For instance, a new crisis of sexual identity often emerges: Am I still truly a man or woman, for I do feel different? Sexual urges are less frequent and less vital, and youth is a constant reminder of age, a fact that this person cannot change. One's crisis is especially acute if a previous identity crisis was not adequately resolved.

Existential depression is also a significant experience. This person more or less experiences the most fundamental loss—loss of meaning. Life seems to make more nonsense than sense; everyone and everything seem distant and not worth attaining. A woman, for instance, is left alone with her meaninglessness and she feels lonely. No one seems able to reach her, and she feels worthless to reach out to anyone, and even though others may offer to help her, she often feels that others have forsaken her. She may feel that she is not worthy to be loved or to give love. How can a person who lacks so much be loved? Life has come to an end. She also feels that she has lost a good portion of her life—a life that she can never relive or regain. Her limits push in on her; she is depressed. In her most acute moments she feels immobile, melancholic, lethargic, guilty, inadequate, and restless. Her mood baffles everyone, including her.

People in her situation, frequently the family, can reinforce her depression often because, although they usually have good intentions, they may try to divert her attention from her depression. They try to get her involved in all kinds of activities or back to her old self—anything except to live the reality that she experiences. Of course, if she runs away from her depression, she runs away from herself, for she is herself in depression.

Furthermore, we usually experience guilt wherein we look at the past life, and forgotten experiences reemerge and plague our conscience. Past actions come back to haunt us and we tend to identify with them. We may condemn ourselves for acts for which we had absolved ourselves in the past. Or we may feel that we are partially responsible for the world's sad condition and that we have done little to make it better. Our ruminating retrospection takes us out of the present and promotes a depressive and guilty withdrawal.

Although the dynamics of no-thingness are basically the same for men and women, there are sexual differences that we cannot pursue in this or in the other stages of no-thingness. One important difference, however, is that a woman in no-thingness is usually more involved with intrapersonal issues. Her menopause forces her to take a new stand toward herself, not only physically but even more psychologically. A woman is more inclined than a man to ask questions oriented within her skin and particularly those centered in her spiritual self. A man also introspects but tends more to focus on his ego functions, so that his work achievements—past, present, and future—are more significant for him than for most women. Although far from being exclusive, his critical eyes are focused more on issues outside his skin.

If this person rejects his no-thingness, he will suffer senselessly. A frequent method of rejection is to get caught in the normal and mad mode of becoming depressed about being depressed. This implies that the person is at odds with himself because he cannot accept his experience, the eventual result being an increase in depression that makes little sense. Thus, this person's attempt to escape from no-thingness results in entrapment. In the extreme but not uncommon case a person may become pathologically depressed, so that he becomes immobilized and falls into despair. However, a temporary destruction can be creative or regressive. For instance, a psychotic involutional depression can be fruitful if it leads to a higher degree of integration. Sometimes a person may emerge as a better and healthier person because he or she has lived and learned from psychotic depression.

If we openly accept our experience and if we can get support from those around us, we will come to new insights, even in no—thingness. We will see the world through depressed eyes that will promote sensitivity to and understanding of experiences, a certain kind of creativity, an appreciation of death and limitedness, and the ability to suffer meaningfully. We will also grow in wisdom wherein we gain a comprehensive perspective; we see things in the light of history and eternity. Things are not likely to seduce us. We are not induced to become too busy. We are open to all points of view and find sense in them. We realize that it is non-sense to play games and that phoniness only leads to self destruction. We come to an equilibrium, a balanced life-style, and life becomes a research project. We research the past and project ourselves into the future; this is our presence to reality. Thus, no—thingness will again lead to a higher degree of maturity and to a new appreciation of things.

Love continues to grow. We now find new meaning in solitude and we seek it, for we discover that solitude offers things that other situations do not. We clearly see the transcendent aspects of love. For instance, a woman knows that she does not have to be physically with a person to love that person. She is also willing to suffer for the Other's sake, as witnessed in her loving tolerance when people are ignorant of realities that she clearly sees. Along with love, her work takes on a deeper meaning. She incorporates work into a comprehensive plan of life so that it becomes an important act among others. She is not seduced into identifying life with her work. She sees more value in being than in the possessions acquired from work. Yet on the job she is more stable and free, a stability that increases her efficiency.

Furthermore, we realize that life is moving toward death, and we do not see death as a distant event to avoid, but we accept it as a present reality. We know that death is not simply an isolated act which people sooner or later experience, but that death is always happening, that we are always in contact with death. We feel and live death's presence as long as we live. We feel death in the experience of our limits, in no—thingness, in wonder, in depression, in anxiety, in dread. We admit that since life and death depend on each other for meaning, the one without the other becomes meaningless. Living the reality of coming to death gives us a deeper appreciation of life.

A man, for instance, enjoys pleasure not just as a matter of sensuality but more as a celebration. Although his body is now quite limited, it takes on new finesse and transcendence. Since he is not so likely to be seduced by the immediacy of his body, it emerges into a transcendent vitality. Pleasurable events become opportunities for celebration—a way of going deeper into reality, not of escaping it.

This person becomes a gentle-man; he is mild and gracious. Even if he is culturally or personally deprived, he attains a certain grace and simplicity of spirit. His spirit vibrates more than ever. It makes its presence known. His spirit fills him with spirit—he is full of life and he enjoys living. His earth becomes a place to celebrate.

Although his suffering is probably greater than ever, this person accepts it more and often makes explicit sense of it. He realizes that pain is an essential part of life and that certain insights into reality are only revealed in pain. He knows that growth without pain is a fiction and that his pain gives him the opportunity for sensitivity, mature suffering, compassion, and love.

In helping people, we draw from the wealth of our experience and keep things in perspective. We realize that a good guide walks with a person and uses motives of appeal. We do not force a person to accept realities that we personally see as valid, but we invite others to see and enjoy the richness of life.

The dark night of the soul also leads us to a new and richer experience of the Holy. Holy experiences complement us and vibrate throughout our behavior. A holy orientation does not mean that we are explicitly and constantly focused on the Holy; in fact, as in our past life, we directly experience the Holy only in special situations. On the other hand, however, our explicit experiences of the Holy do increase in frequency and quality, and our implicit presence to the Holy becomes more and more present in the foreground of everyday behavior. Although we are involved in life with much more authority and responsibility and are more accountable and responsible than ever before, our behavior is permeated with love.

We emerge from depressive and guilty no-thingness to the ground of life—the Other. If we do not find or renew our ultimate concern of holiness, we will get caught in the death of depression or will try to escape from no-thingness. The holy person in this involutional stage faces death and finds life, and his or her no-thingness is fulfilled by the human and holy Other.

NO–THINGNESS IN OLD AGE

With the exception of death, the last critical stage of no-thingness occurs in the second half of the sixties or later, usually after retirement. Our body is much weaker than in the past and is rapidly becoming weaker. Reflexes have slowed down; eating and sleeping habits have changed. Although physical activity can and should be maintained, the body cannot be actualized as much and as vigorously as before. This person as ego is no longer involved as he or she used to be, for usually we are no longer working professionally. Our paramount point is that the functions and values of the body and ego become less and less significant in contrast to the functions and values of the spirit. The spirit takes over more than ever, for we are left in time primarily with our spiritual self.

Usually our situation changes radically. If a worker has retired, he (or she) must now learn, to a large degree, a new way of life. He may suddenly find that he has time on his hands and he does not know what to do. He no longer has to go to work. It is up to him to make his time meaningful. A homemaker must make a new adjustment, for a homemaker is suddenly left with more time with a spouse, and this has never happened before. The situation has fundamentally changed by the very presence of the spouse. If widowed, more often she finds herself alone. This person must find new friends or find old friends in a new way. No longer can she expect the companionship of her spouse; no longer can she depend on the daily routines the spouse provided. A single person may have no-thing even more acutely. A single person too often has to face her lonely no-thingness alone. Even if this person lives in a community, she finds that many of her friends have died or have left and she is in a different situation, such as a retirement home. Regardless of the particular situation, the old person must go out into the world anew.

Death is directly in front of this person; death is impossible to deny. Many friends and relatives may have already died, and youth are a constant reminder of age. A woman, for example, feels death more and more in her body, and task-oriented behavior of ego makes less sense. Depression emerges to various degrees and for various reasons, for this person feels that she is losing herself. She may also experience a loss of self-esteem in the loss of bodily and functional powers. Her life is nearing its end, and she begins to reflect on it. Since she naturally sees life in perspective and realizes that she cannot live it over again, she is forced to accept what has happened. She no longer has the energy to run away from death—death has caught her.

Western culture makes it especially difficult for this person to accept no-thingness. Since people in Western culture are judged on their ability to produce and if one can no longer produce, he or she is seen as a burden—someone to remove from the mainstream of life. People in the Western culture seldom listen to older people. Elders are, at best, people to tolerate. Geriatric sections of hospitals and homes for the aged are often living testimonies to this perverted view of old age. Too often old people are placed in geriatric hospitals, not because they need psychiatric or medical help, but because they interfere with the lives of younger people. Even old people are conditioned to think that they are a burden, in the way, a nuisance. They reluctantly withdraw so that they do not interfere with the lives of their children. A paradox exists for this is often when children are ready to give to their parents materially in terms of bodily comfort and financial security, but not spiritually in terms of love, care, understanding, and appreciation. These experiences are the very ones an old person needs, yet they are the ones that are withheld.

How the aged person accepts and lives through no-thingness depends largely on his or her previous life-decisions and experiences of no-thingness. If a person has made healthy options toward past critical experiences, this period of no-thingness can be relatively easy but nevertheless painful. For instance, if a woman has already gone through the crisis of the limits successfully, she is likely to accept this stage. Here she dwells in no—thingness and gains insight in herself and in life and death. She will come to a new level of wisdom and higher integration.

Her life takes on its deepest meaning, and her love really becomes transcendent. She does not need the constant reassurance of sex to affirm her love, and she knows that she can still deeply love the dead, who live in her appreciation of death. She is glad to be left with a lot of time, for she enjoys this time to live. Life can no longer bother her—she is too close to death and life. Her body and ego demands may bring pain, but not stress. She sees life in the light of death, and this lived insight makes her life take on a new vibrancy. By accepting death, she becomes full of life.

On the other hand, a person who does not renew himself in no—thingness usually falls into a depressive stagnation. He becomes depressed about being depressed, tired of being tired, bored with being bored, sick of being sick, and weak about being weak. This person fights himself, and since he has little energy, he wastes away. Initially, this person will often try to find things to do to fill his time and no—thingness. But after a short time, he is left with himself in no—thingness; he has no—thing. Faced with no—thing and not knowing how to accept and face himself, he identifies with no—thing. Thus, he becomes restive and restless. Depression overwhelms him, and he disintegrates into no—thingness. Eventually, this person kills himself—physically or psychologically.

This is the time when a person can re-create and celebrate life, for she has the time and, above all, the knowledge and wisdom. Even if society does reject her by tolerating her, she can still transcend her situation. However, if a person's life is closely unidentified with her function in life, when he or she retires, this person retires from life and not just from her function in life. Consequently, it behooves an older person to prepare for retirement long before it is time to be retired. A person does not adjust just by wishing it so. Preparation should be mainly internal—a solid evaluation of personal values. For example, the values of having and doing mean less in retirement; being predominates. Also, interests like learning how to enjoy and celebrate everyday activities such as walking, eating, talking, and traveling can be crucially significant. Individual interests like reading, music, sports, and social activities can also help a person to enjoy time in a meaningful way.

We have mentioned that if a person has identified life with work, he or she will lose that life. On the other hand, psychological and cultural influences make work crucially important for most retirees. Life without any work can be critical in itself. In this light, it is usually helpful to find some part-time work within and/or outside the home. Our main point is that retirees learn to enjoy work; to see it not as a burdensome task but as a pleasant and meaningful activity.

If the Holy does not emerge in a person's sixties, death will probably occur prematurely. Death will manifest itself initially in the spiritual realm, then psychologically, and finally biologically. This person will be left without any saving meaning in life: ultimate concern will be present only in its absence. He will find it impossible to live without a ground for being, so that the time he has will be time for no-thing. No longer can he escape from his yearning for the Holy. The Holy has caught up to him in time. This person can no longer use the weak functions of his body and ego as self escapes, for without a meaningful and ultimate ground his ego becomes useless and his body feels no sense in living.

Although a tragedy, this crisis can be prolonged into the seventies and longer. Because of certain situational factors, an old person may be suspended in a nebulous field of no-thingness. People, at home or away from home, may unconsciously help an old person to maintain himself in no-thingness, and although they prevent him from dying with minimal institutional care, they seldom take time to listen to or to talk with an old person. In helpless collusion, an old person may play the game of being old (sick, useless, and dependent) and slowly dissipate in no-thingness.

If a person has repressed the Holy in his or her past, it becomes very difficult to admit the Holy; however, it is not impossible. This person must be willing to suffer in order to rekindle the repressed years of no-thingness before being liberated to and for the Holy. One must be willing to pay the price of self-denial in terms of depression, guilt, and loneliness. On the other hand, a person who has lived through no-thingness and has found the holy ground of life will find it relatively easy to reach a climax of holiness. Explicit encounters with the Holy will be more and more permeated with the Holy. This elder's time is filled with meaning, living more and more in an overt state of holiness. This person gladly accepts the encounters of no-thingness and realizes the deepest and richest experience of love. Life will become a constant celebration of the human and holy Other.

Finally, a holy old person is beautiful. She or he may frighten people in that holiness and oldness are not congruent with a production-centered culture. Others may try to disregard this beautiful elder, but to do so takes effort. Even though little is spoken, the silent holiness speaks for itself. One of Western culture's greatest faults is that people seldom listen to the wisdom and holiness of healthy old people. These old people disclose the pathology of Western culture in witnessing to the wholeness and holiness that are lacking in the culture.

FINAL NO-THINGNESS

The final encounter with no-thingness comes in death. A dying person faces the meaninglessness of chaos and the meaningfulness of order. Whether or not the Holy fulfills a person's no-thingness depends on how he or she prepared for this moment of life. It seems reasonable to conclude that if death (losses, change, no-thingness, deserts) has led to life (gains, stability, being, promised lands), then the final time of death will lead to perpetual life.

Death's grand finale will usher in life's epiphany. Finally, the depression, loneliness, and anxiety of no-thingness will engender everlasting joy, love, and serenity. We will return from where we came—to rest in peace, without pain, eternally together in Love.

4   Our Displacement of the Holy

WE HAVE SEEN that if we emerge from no–thingness, we come to a deeper and more meaningful experience of reality. We will find the ground of our being—love for and from the human and holy Other. However, what happens when a person does not accept no–thingness and consequently the Other? Our concern in this chapter is to answer these questions by proposing that we replace the Other with substitute objects primarily to fulfill and escape from no–thingness. Although it is important to study our displacement of people, our accent in this chapter is on our displacement of the holy Other rather than the human Other. However, we emphasize that a displacement of the Holy eventually and necessarily leads to a displacement of self and others. Before presenting some common and concrete modes of displacement, we will begin with a more general and abstract picture of our displacement of the Holy.

DISPLACEMENT OF THE HOLY

Theoretically, the process of displacement refers to a distortion of the appropriate goal of a motive whereby a person replaces the true but inaccessible or threatening goal with a substitute object. A classic example is the working man who for various reasons cannot directly express his anger toward his boss, who originally evoked the anger. Arriving home, he immediately becomes angry with his unsuspecting wife. In this case the wife acts as the substitute object that replaces the true but inaccessible goal of his anger—the boss. Energy that was originally directed toward a specific situation (toward his boss) is now invested or expressed in a substitute situation (toward his wife). Thus, instead of openly admitting to his anger toward his boss, the husband tends to repress what he would really like to do, and his "angry energy" is "let out" on his wife. Although he gets some relief from his displaced expression, he not only exploits his wife but he also prevents himself from owning up to and understanding his feelings toward his boss.

In a similar manner, we can repress or distort our movement toward the human and holy Other by replacing the Other with a substitute object. In this case, our desire or "energy" is not directed toward its proper goal—the Holy—but is displaced in a substitute activity. It is emphasized that when we displace the Holy we try to satisfy our desire and thereby gain a sense of fulfillment. In fact, a displacement of the Holy can and often does make sense. We escape from our nothingness and gain a precarious and temporary fulfillment. The substitute activity does fulfill us, although it is an inadequate fulfillment. However, the contradiction remains. We can never actualize ourselves, for we do not admit the proper object of our innate desire. In our attempt to become whole we displace the Holy and become unwhole.

Another important point is that a displacement implicitly refers to the object that originally evoked the response. The husband, who inappropriately displaced his anger on his wife, betrayed the goal of his angry motive—his boss. In addition, he is encumbered with guilt and shame. If his wife were to wait for a while, she would be able to discover the real reason for her husband's annoyance, that is, the proper object of his anger—his boss. Likewise, the displacement of a person's holy desire implicitly refers to the Holy, since the displacement is an attempt to fulfill the need for the Holy.

Thus, our futile attempts to displace the Holy are indications of the Holy in its absence, and our methods of hiding the Holy betray our desire for the Holy. Our task is to discover and to rekindle the Holy hidden in the displaced activities. Otherwise, we contend that we will lose the Other and ourselves and consequently lead a meaningless existence.

We have seen that a yearning to be fulfilled exists initially and most acutely in the experience of no-thingness. I experience a desire to be fulfilled—to be something, to be someone, to be myself. I want to find existential meaning in life and to achieve a sense of well-being and happiness. Since only love can fulfill me, love for and from the Holy and people, I must let the Holy reveal itself. However, the desire for the Holy is absent, repressed, rejected, or hidden in too many people. In our attempt to make sense out of life a person might displace the Holy, becoming neither whole nor holy. If we reject the Holy, certain consequences emerge.

Most fundamentally we lose the ground for our existence. We search desperately for something to give us a valid orientation—a solid ground in which to root life. We constantly try to discover something that will fulfill our no-thingness and make us be ourselves. We do not realize that only the Other, including the Holy, can fulfill us. Since we do not or cannot let the Holy save us from our no-thingness, our search for meaning leads to meaninglessness.

Although we do reach a sense of meaningful wholeness in displacement activities, it is temporary and inadequate. We develop into a lived contradiction. Our striving for ground leaves us groundless. Since our efforts to be whole preclude the Holy, we are left fragmented, and our displacement of the Holy leads to a personal displacement. We cannot find our place in life, for we cannot live the fact that our place is to love self, others, and the Holy. We fail to realize that we can be wholly ourselves only by giving ourselves to others and to the Holy. Thus, our rejection of the holy Other leads to a rejection of our self and the human Other. Furthermore, our activity for replacing the Holy is itself perverted and displaced because our activity is made to satisfy a need (for the Holy) that is outside its realm. For example, when sex is used to satisfy the need for love, not only is the Other displaced but the sexual act itself is exploited and therefore perverted. Thus, a circular causality is promoted. Our attempts for fulfillment via displacement become less and less fulfilling and simultaneously promote a greater need for meaningful fulfillment.

The displaced person constantly feels incomplete and guilty. Our incompleteness does not stem from our dynamic restlessness, but from our fragmentation. We feel that an important part of life is missing, for we experience the Holy in its absence, and our sense of not being whole leads to guilt. Although we are usually not conscious of what we are guilty about, guilt permeates our existence.

Other experiences also emerge from the rejection of the Holy. We become existentially frustrated, for our existence is basically blocked from further self emergence. We also become chronically depressed in that we have lost fundamental meaning in life. Our loss is not of this or that person, but is more fundamentally a loss of the Other. Furthermore, displacements ultimately serve to exacerbate depression. The more we displace, the more we become depressed.

Being displaced, we are bored. Our frantic boring into life for meaning results in a subtle but fundamental sense of tiredness. We become sick and tired of searching, and because of a lack of meaning we become bored to death with life. Everything becomes boring. Things often become ends in themselves and lose their meaning without the Holy. A lack of ultimate concern makes life sterile and helpless, since there are few possibilities for lasting fulfillment. Boredom often leads to a lived despair wherein life makes no fundamental sense, and lived despair may lead to ultimate despair—death. Since there is no sense in living, death becomes the only solution to meaninglessness.

It might appear that the displaced person's experiences are the same as the experiences of a person in no–thingness. Indeed, there are similarities because both people are in no–thingness, though in different ways. Displaced persons try to escape from no–thingness instead of living through it. In fact, they are chronically afraid of no–thingness, and their displacement of the Other is a futile and frantic attempt to escape from the vortex of no–thingness. Since they run constantly and anxiously from being lost in no–thingness, they lose everything. Their experiences of loneliness, anxiety, depression, etc., do not promote discovery, growth, and meaningfulness; on the contrary, they are indicative of adequacy, maintenance, and meaninglessness. Since displaced people do not openly admit that they are their experiences, their escape from "them" is also an escape from themselves. On the other hand, people who accept their experiences in no–thingness find themselves and the Other.

If we do find ourselves in this bind of meaninglessness, why do we refuse to accept no–thingness? It is meaningful for us to review some of the reasons for escaping from no–thingness. We saw that the experience of no–thingness is a painful experience, and most people are conditioned to reject pain. They try to live according to a pleasure principle, that is, a lack-of-pain principle. Westerners automatically try to get rid of pain because it is non-sense to them, and at best they merely tolerate it.

We also find ourselves alone, lonely, empty, yearning, limited, depressed, lost, anxious, and nothing. All these experiences are not supported by the culture or by most people. The cultural value system of production and pleasure is incongruent with these experiences. Seldom are we given permission to be, support in being, and affirmation of being left alone in no–thingness. Fur-thermore, people are afraid of possible chaos in no–thingness and therefore have a compulsive need to make order of things. For these and for many individual reasons, it becomes difficult for us to accept our no–thingness.

There are several kinds of persons who have difficulty with no–thingness. Immature persons do not willfully reject their yearn-ing for the Holy, because they have never really had the oppor-tunity to experience no–thingness. Although children can be mature for their age, they are too immature to encounter the Holy directly. They are in a process of not-yetness in regard to the Holy. Although their immaturity may be due to an impover-ished environment or they may be fixated at an earlier stage of development, immature adults have never really reached the level of development wherein they can confront the Holy as a mature adult. Nevertheless, they can come to a simple presence to the Holy. Although mentally retarded persons may not have much ego ability to support and promote their yearning in no–thingness, they too may come to a pure but undifferentiated holy experience.

On the other hand, neurotic people may try to repress their desire for the Holy, and consequently they live an anxious existence. Since they are unconsciously forced to use various defense mechanisms to repress their holy desire, they fight a losing battle. The more they repress, the stronger their desire becomes. They live in a state of unawareness and of being out of touch with themselves. Unlike neurotics, persons of bad faith willfully reject the Holy and consciously promote displacement of the Holy for their own benefit. A person of bad faith who says no to the Holy is fundamentally willful, whereas the neurotic's negation is basically unconscious. However, neurotic people may not close themselves to the Holy, although they do repress other important experiences. They live neurotic yet holy lives.

Psychotic people may experience the Holy in an undifferentiated, primitive way especially in the initial and acute phases of psychosis. Since psychosis is usually some kind of ego disintegration, it does not necessarily preclude spiritual processes, which may include a psychotic experience of the Holy. Since psychotic people have little ego control, other experiences intermingle and infringe on their holy experience. Their experience becomes increasingly confused, for the more chronic the psychosis, the more self-disintegration results. Thus, in time, this psychotic person, too, risks losing contact with the Holy.

If psychotic persons did have holy experiences before their illness, they may have more intense but more confusing experiences of the Holy in their psychotic mode of existence. In fact, a psychotic experience may be fruitful in that one may come to a fuller appreciation of the Holy in and through a psychotic experience and in that a psychotic disintegration is in service of a future and a healthier reintegration. A rejection of the Holy may also result in a psychotic episode wherein one is forced to face oneself and the Holy. However, not all psychotic persons experience the Holy, for a person may be too immature, regressed, disintegrated, or repressed to be capable of this experience.

The most common type of person who displaces the Holy is the normal person. Although normal persons are not mentally ill, they are not healthy. By satisfying their basic needs, they are able to maintain themselves and prevent unhealthiness. They manage to adjust to reality by giving the minimum demanded by self and the Other. On the other hand, normal persons do not actualize themselves and the Other to the fullest possible degree, nor is the Holy a constant and consistent ultimate concern. Many normal people lead a marginal existence in that they maintain peripheral contact with the Holy by such activities as passively attending liturgical services, by routine prayer, and by appeal to the Holy in times of want. However, the Holy is not the main motivating force in their lives, but is more like a fringe benefit. Although normal people do not willfully promote displacement of the Holy, they may find themselves displacing the Holy because of such factors as personality needs, environmental stress, and cultural pressures. The paramount point is that they try to escape from no-thingness by replacing the Holy with substitute objects, resulting in a normal and meaningless life. Their attempt to fulfill themselves without the Holy is a normal form of madness. Some of these normal modes of madness—displacements of the Holy—are the subjects for our next analyses.

POWERISM

"Powerism" is a neologism that refers to a lifestyle of people who invest their desire for the Holy in power. These persons transform their will to the Holy into a will-to-power, and consequently they operate primarily according to the will-to-power. Power is a valid and necessary mode of functioning, but when power becomes the central motivating force, it becomes "powerism."

Such power people make themselves the center of the universe; they see themselves as the most important reality. Rather than orienting their life toward the Other, they demand that life center around them. Instead of becoming allocentric, they become egocentric. Since most of their time and energy is invested in their ego processes, their ultimate concern is their own ego. Ego values become their ultimate values; reflective thinking and choosing, adjustment, control, objectivity, organization, etc., are primary. Life is a business for these people; their lives become fully immersed in their organizational identity.

As a power person I try to be completely independent and to control everything. Since I operate almost exclusively on an ego level, I tend to be coldly efficient and superficial. I do not accept limits in self or in others, because I want to be perfect; in fact, I want to be God. My approach is based on what I think should happen. I have only to push the proper button and things will happen. My body is controlled unless I decide to indulge in bodily pleasure, for bodies—my own and others'—are only means toward an end. I also repress my spirit, for faith, risk, mystery, paradox, etc., are too threatening and are beyond control. I cannot afford to admit them. Experiences that are ends in themselves are meaningless, for everything is conditional and a means toward something else. The end is myself. We can say that I try to redeem myself from my no-thingness because I alone try to make myself something.

Since I deify myself, I think I know what is best for everyone.

In my closed presence to others I impose my own frame of reference on them. My approach is in terms of either/or. I will never admit to paradox or ambiguity. Since I am not truly capable of considering the other person's viewpoint, it is impossible for me to understand. Actually, I see interpersonal relationships in terms of "conquest" because my life depends on "winning."

It makes sense to operate according to the will-to-power. Since I think that I have control over everything, I need not be afraid of nothing. My mastery over the world and others gives me a certain sense of security. Moreover, I know exactly where I stand, and since I control the Other, the Other cannot threaten me. I gain a sense of solidarity and certainty in my willfulness, and often others initially give me a kind of affirmation. They admire my efficiency and objectivity or they may sense the strength in my ego willpower. From this frame of reference, my primary gain is to escape from no-thingness. I fulfill myself with things, and my control of everything prevents me from falling away into no-thingness. In fact, I do temporarily escape the pain, loneliness, and depression of no-thingness.

There are a number of individual reasons why a person escapes from no-thingness and displaces the Holy with power. A rather common reason is that my will-to-power is a reaction formation against my unconscious feelings of helplessness and inadequacy. I overcompensate for my weakness in facing myself and life. Since I have learned to reject myself and consequently have no faith in myself, I replace the certitude of faith with the certainty of thinking. Often my sexual identity is tenuous, and consequently my interpersonal relationships are precarious. Since my lifestyle is a constant compensation for repressed feelings of inadequacy, I am always forced to be certain of everything.

My mode of existence is a tragic self-deception, for my escape from no-thingness results in an escape from myself. I become more and more fragmented and alienated, and my efficiency slowly and progressively dissipates. While I am young, my ego strength is sufficient to adjust and be skillful, but in the crisis of my thirties I experience my first vestiges of weakness not only in body but also in ego mind. With each crisis of no-thingness I become more and more threatened, and more and more compulsive to be in control. I begin to live in a state of panic. No-thingness—the one experience I cannot control—is always present.

I quickly lose the respect I once had from others; for others find me coldly obnoxious, and they begin to withdraw from me. I become lonely, bored, and disgusted. The very experiences I have tried to escape from are slowly catching up to me. I may try to escape into such activities as drinking or compulsive domination. But in time, no-thingness catches me, if not in the no-thingness of middle age, then in the crisis of old age. Finally, I have nothing to control.

I find myself in a bind because the only approaches I know—control and manipulation—do not work. Thus, I fight myself in not accepting the experiences emergent from no-thingness. Depression, loneliness, anxiety, and meaninglessness flood in on me. Since I have conditioned myself into rejecting nothing, I get caught in the chaos of no-thingness, and my dream of controlling everything leaves me as a no-thing.

Things lose their meaning and they no longer give Secure satisfaction. Spiritual experiences are absent, and there is no transcendent meaning in life. Religious values are nonsense, and the Other is inaccessible. I am left in no-thingness with my crumbling ego, which is useless in regard to the mystery of nothing.

119

Ultimately I am caught in the quagmire of a meaningless and groundless existence. I lose control, and life begins to overwhelm me. Since I cannot affirm my no-thingness, I cannot encounter the Holy; and the more I try to control, the more I repress myself and the Other. In fact, the more I control, the less control I eventually have. I become a broken and lost person, for my will-to-power has left me will-less.

In the final analysis, I am left with nothing but myself; since I have alienated myself from the Other, I lack the ground of transcendence, and everything becomes boring. My displacement of the Holy into power has left me powerless and helpless to live meaningfully.

Although my situation is very difficult, I am not hopeless. Sometimes I experience an involutional depression wherein I find the opportunity to explore new horizons. I may come to accept no-thingness and to be liberated from my compulsion to control things. Through my acceptance of nothing I become free enough to direct my desire for the Holy to the Holy. I begin to own up to what I am instead of becoming something I am not. On the other hand, I may never come to admit my no-thingness, so that I fail to confront the Other in their life and continue to lead a groundless existence. Instead of becoming a powerful god, I eventually end up a helpless nothing.

WORKISM

When work is the highest value in one's hierarchy of values, it serves as the central motivating force in a person's life and becomes "workism." Since work is primary and everything else is of secondary importance, life is seen in the light of work, not of love.

Being a workaholic, I identify my life with my work, and in Marcelian terms I become a "functional man." Since I also operate primarily according to the ego processes, I am frequently and closely related to the power person. (The willpower person may also be a functional man by investing willpower in work.) Organization, planning, analyzing, thinking, coping, efficiency, and other ego processes are primary; similar to the will-to-power persons, I am devoid of spiritual values. I use my body in work, but seldom enjoy my body; and I have no time for spiritual and body experiences, for life is work.

However, I am not as cold and efficiently barbaric as is the willpower person. I am a hard worker and often I am more flexible and more understanding, especially at work. In fact, people admire and resent me for my work and pity me for my life. I earnestly work myself to death without truly experiencing life.

I become so busy that life passes me by. I have no time to live, only time to work, and I eventually lose personal contact with the human and holy Other. For instance, I have no sense of recreation. Play is a waste of time, and vacations are means of recuperating for work, not a way of vacating the routine life in order to be and to recreate. Or, I may work at playing, so that my compulsiveness to enjoy myself is a contradiction to the nature of play. Even in sexuality I work. If I take the time, I use techniques exclusively to gain maximum enjoyment. My entire life is task-oriented, and my work is a world of labor exclusive of the worlds of play, aesthetics, pleasure, and love.

Many people get caught in the bind of workism. For instance, a woman who lives according to the values of *having* instead of those of *being* must necessarily work overtime because her life is based on possession, not on the Other and herself. She must make more and more money in order to have more, but she cannot afford to ask what her having is for. Her possessions become ends in themselves, and yet she takes no time to enjoy them. In this situation, money is also made a displacement that is usually an attempt to hold on to things in order to escape from no-thingness. Money enables this person to run from life instead of serving her as a means of going deeper into life. Money becomes an end in itself and the most important end. In time, however, money becomes meaningless, and the person is left with no-thingness. This person slowly realizes that money does not help in no-thingness, life, and death.

Another example is the clergyman who identifies his life with his work. His life centers around his profession instead of around his commitment to the Holy. Thus, when a church or a school is threatened with being closed, his own existence is threatened. He asks himself not only what he is going to do but also what he is going to be. The fact that he has made himself into a professional and is not a holy person is resented. People begin to lose respect for the clergy and begin to feel that they are phonies. The clergyman often misinterprets this attitude and works even harder to prove himself to the world through work. Little does he realize that the layman wants him to be himself—primarily a holy person and secondarily a worker.

Life centered around work makes sense for many reasons. For instance, if a person has come from a poor environment or has lived through the throes of an economic depression, he or she may be overly anxious about possessions in order to gain some security and dignity. Or a person who compulsively keeps up with the Joneses may be trying to gain a sense of worth from having things instead of from within oneself. Workism is also congruent with the culture that values a person's worth on the basis of his production rate. Furthermore, the pressure of contemporary living demands much money in that the cost to shelter, clothe, feed, and educate a family adequately is high. In short, the Zeitgeist is conducive to the workaholic.

Most important, work fulfills one's no-thingness. Workism enables a person to escape temporarily from the unworkable pain of no-thingness. I need not be anxious about no-things; work gives me a bearing in life, something to hold on to, and results. Work also helps to maintain me physically, economically, and psychologically, so that after a good day's work I feel completed and satisfied. I feel like somebody—like a good worker. Often I am too tired to worry about no-thingness, for when I work, eat, and sleep, there is no time for no-thingness. Work makes sense; no-thing is nonsense. My work—not the Holy-gives me ultimate meaning in life. I become "a worker," not an authentic person.

My main crisis usually occurs in retirement because, since I have identified life with work, I retire from life when I retire from work. I am left with what I have conditioned myself to reject—no-thing. Initially I search frantically for work around the house, but this work is not the same. Furthermore, my age limits me, because the more I try to work, the more fatigued I become. Soon I am left with time on my hands and I do not know what to do with it; life becomes boring. Although my crisis of no-thingness is close, I still try to escape because I do not know how to accept it. The no-thingness of death shakes the ground of my existence. I become progressively tired, bored, depressed, and lonely; and finally I am caught in no-thingness.

Although it is possible, especially with support, to live through my no-thingness and find life, it is more likely that I will die—

psychologically and prematurely biologically. Too often I want holy meaning in life, but I am unable to find the Holy in and through my no-thingness. I slowly waste away, for my work displacement of the Holy has been taken away and I am frightened to death by the call of the Holy in no-thingness.

Although a woman may suffer more, she is usually more able to accept and to cope with this crisis of no-thingness. Since most women live a communal-centered life, they do not experience as sudden a change in lifestyle as do men. However, it is more difficult for a woman who is a professional person, because then the syndrome of experiences is similar to the man's. Indeed, the sudden and constant presence of a woman's husband changes her situation. Besides wondering what she is going to do with him, this woman also comes into a new way of living. Her children have grown and probably live elsewhere so that suddenly she is left alone with her husband. If she has displaced the Holy with her work in the house and with her children, she too comes to a retirement crisis. If both parties have displaced the Other, they are left with themselves and they may discover that they have grown to be strangers to each other. If they refuse to accept the gift of the Other in no-thingness, life becomes worthless, and instead of seeing this as a time to love and enjoy each other, they grow more distant and die.

Work as the ultimate concern is doomed to dissipate, for work is basically a means toward greater ends. Thus, work is an inappropriate answer to our yearning for the Other. Only the human and holy Other can give us life, including our work, fundamental meaning and ground.

THEORISM

Theorism is another neologism used to refer to a rather common displacement, particularly for the person in his or her twenties or thirties. Theorism means that persons make a system of thought or a particular theory their ultimate concern, so that they live more in a theoretical world than in the experiential world. They see their theory as being the main source of truth and tend to absolutize their theory to the exclusion of experience and other theories.

Theorism is primarily a function of the ego, because the ego is the level of theory construction. The theoretician reflects on experience and then tries to make sense of reality by means of a theory. Theory is an intellectual construction that approximates experience from a particular viewpoint. Although theories are necessary in order to comprehend explicitly the structure and functions of reality, an important point is that theory presupposes experience and should be in the service of experience. When a theory becomes a substitute for experience, the theory becomes theorism.

An advocate of theorism distorts or denies any experience that is not congruent with his or her theory. Instead of theory being in service of experience, my experience is forced to be in service of theory. I live primarily in my mind, not in life. Theory becomes a displacement of the lived-world, including the holy experience. The kind of theorism that a person adopts is usually compensation for unsatisfied and unconscious needs. A needy person may choose from among several forms of theories, some of which will be discussed in the following paragraphs.

Psychology can be idolized and used to fulfill a person's no-thingness. Often some forms of psychology may seem more meaningful than forms of other sciences or of religion. Psychology particularly appeals to persons who have repressed their affective life, because psychology and psychotherapy may give them a needed opportunity to express themselves. They see psychology as being more in harmony with their experience than other approaches to life. Their psychological orientation gives them a sense of liberation from their past repressed life, and life seems to come alive through psychology really for the first time.

For instance, sensitivity training—a group dynamic approach—may liberate people who have never really been in experiential touch with themselves and with life in general. This group process can be excellent if it serves as an appropriate way to become in touch with life. However, it can be destructive if the group is not led by a qualified leader and if it is engaged in for the wrong reasons. Various forms of group process too often appeal to needy people who unconsciously see the group as a panacea for their personal problems or as a means for instant fulfillment. Or, too often people are forced to experience feelings for which they are not ready or for which they do not really choose. At other times, the group function may turn into psychological and mutual masturbation. These groups can be greedily taken as a displacement of the Holy, particularly for the lost and unfulfilled person who is searching for significant meaning.

Another related danger is to play psychological games. Such persons begin to "psychologize" about life—every action has a psychological reason. Figuring out people gives them a decided advantage and a consequent sense of power and security. Psychologizing might also help them to justify any behavior for the sake of having the experience, behaving on the premise: if it feels right, it is right.

For this reason, psychology makes more sense than the Holy. Psychologism is made the ultimate value and central motive in life. Psychology is not seen as a means of liberating us for an encounter with the Holy and with others. If another person does not fit into the psychological theory, the Other is rejected or made to feel guilty. The Other is sacrificed for the sake of psychology.

I can also displace the Holy with a philosophical theory, stating that truth is found in philosophy, not in life. For instance, a philosophical system may give clear and distinct ideas of the Holy which give me a false security in knowing exactly where I stand. My system may give me exact and clear standards for behavior, so that I do not have to worry about doubt, paradox, and crisis. Life is no longer a mystery. I know everything and I need not bother with no–thing.

Too often my metaphysical notion of the Holy is based on an antiquated philosophy that made sense centuries ago but does not necessarily make sense for contemporary experience. For example, I may give priority to conceptual instead of experiential knowledge of love, or I may see the Holy as the one who is always above oneself and consequently can be contacted only in solitude and not in and through people. I may constantly "talk" about love of God and neighbor, but I seldom "live" these Commandments concretely in day-to-day behavior. Since my philosophy primarily hides truth instead of revealing it, I actually do a disservice to philosophy and to myself. Later in life I find it impossible to love a God of metaphysics. I discover that my concept of the Holy is different from my experience of the Holy. I may even find that my love for my concept of the Holy was to some extent self idolatry (as criticized so well by the proponents of the "projection approach" toward God).

Actually, we can adopt any theoretical system as a displacement of the Holy and therefore of life. Theology, psychology, sociology, anthropology, philosophy, etc., can be absolutized and lived as the ultimate concern in life. For instance, when I consider that the only relevant truth comes from the positive sciences, I become an advocate of scientism. The scientistic person thinks that every experience eventually can be understood and controlled by the positive sciences. I analyze the holy experience as a myth or a wish fulfillment that emerged in the past, unscientific times because of our helplessness and insecurity. According to scientism, persons informed by science need not depend on God, but can depend on science for the meaningful and ultimate ground of existence. Thus, scientism displaces the Holy. When a system of thinking is absolutized, the theory is perverted because its lifeline with experience is cut. The "logos" becomes an "ism."

All theories have truth and make sense. However, when "the" truth is made into "the" truth, the theory becomes theorism. The theory becomes my highest value, and experience takes second place. Since I tend to meet others in terms of theory instead of meeting the concrete person, I never really engage the Other, although I may talk about dialogue constantly. In fact, I become somewhat schizoid in becoming entrapped in theory and cut off from experience.

When I live theory instead of life, I usually come to my first great crisis in middle age. I was able to fulfill my no-thingness with theoretical truth in the past. I felt sure that I had "the truth," but my crisis of the limits throws me into no-thingness and forces me to see the limits of my theory. My experience in no-thingness appeals to me to look at the inadequacy of theory in respect to life. I may feel that I have been out of touch with the lived world for a long time and I wonder how I can come back into life. In fact, it is common to observe a theoretician change his or her vested interest after he or she has gone through the crisis of the limits. For instance, the strict scientists begin to ask new questions, questions with a philosophical and a religious flavor, and the common person begins to look for the experiential God rather than for the theoretical God.

Although I may be able to escape from no-thingness into theory even in the crisis of the limits, it becomes increasingly difficult to sustain a theoretical existence. Age tends to keep one honest. It is very rare to see old people playing theoretical games. It simply does not pay as it once did in the past. As always, no-thingness does catch up with me. If a person has only theory to fall back on, I am left with the experience of no-thingness and I become helpless. Experience overwhelms theory, and furthermore, I am tired of using theory. What good does theory do in death?

SEXUALISM

Sexualism is sexuality taken as one's ultimate concern. In this context, sexuality refers to one mode of sexuality—genital sex, actions that directly involve the genital organs and that directly lead to genital behavior. Although genital intercourse is the zenith of genital sexuality, other forms of sexuality, such as heavy petting, are also included in this discussion. Sexualism is a common displacement of the Holy, particularly in the second, third, and fourth decades of life.

A person who displaces the Holy with sex lives according to a sex principle: sex gives me ultimate satisfaction and meaning in life. Sex becomes my central motivating force, and other values and behaviors are subordinate to it. I work, play, and in general live for sex, so that when I am asked what I would most like to do, "Experience sex" is my answer. All my actions are in some way colored by my chief concern—achievement of sexual pleasure. I am concerned for the Other insofar as I can get sexual satisfaction. I am indeed a child who plays—plays with myself—and with others for my own pleasure.

I live primarily according to the sexual values of my body. I live for the moment. Since I want gratification here and now, long-ranged values are absent. I live according to my bodily desires and will use every means to satisfy them. Suffering makes no sense to me, and as soon as I experience pain, such as the stress of no-thingness, I escape into sex. Values of the spirit are not expedient, for they demand a respect for the Other.

Both man and woman can become experts in the "game of sex." A man might use his ego as a means of achieving his sexual ends in knowing what to say and when to say it. For instance, he learns that many women are seduced by dependent honesty, neediness, and frustration, and he plays these roles. Or, he may become an expert in being sensitive to lonely women—women who will do anything for some kind of comfort. The woman also plays the sexual game, as when she learns how to present herself in an erotic but safe way. She quickly learns how to excite the male, how to play with his guilt and responsibility, and how to make him think that he is seducing her. It is often true that the man who thinks that he has "made" the woman discovers that he was "made" sometime ago.

Men and women often play another kind of sexual game that involves an implicit contract to satisfy one another, and although the mutual agreement is seldom overt, it is nevertheless real. The contract is made on the basis of one's own satisfaction—not on giving. They communicate to each other: if you satisfy me, then I'll satisfy you. Since a person as body is centripetal, he or she takes without any notion of giving for the Other's sake; thus, their sexual dialogue is narcissistic.

Sexualism as a displacement for the Holy makes sense primarily because a basic dynamic of sexuality is fulfillment. If I am escaping from no-thingness and I am necessarily looking for an ultimate concern, sex is a most accessible and fulfilling displacement. Whether this sexualism is with another person or with oneself, it fulfills our no-thingness for several reasons.

Sexual fulfillment incorporates satisfaction. The etymology of "satisfaction" indicates that the person is put at rest in sexuality. It takes away my tension and makes me feel at peace. Sexuality also offers me a certain completeness in saying that I have given myself. At the moment of sexual climax, I experience the completeness for which I constantly search; perhaps in no other way can I find completion. I feel that every fiber in my being is activated. I feel whole. Sex makes a lot of sense to a person who is leading a stressful and meaningless life, for in sex I can feel completely at ease without worrying about the throes of my life.

I may be capable of being totally involved only in sex, and if I usually feel out of tune with life, sex can give me a feeling of being grounded. The lonely college sophomore may welcome sexuality as a meaningful relief from her no-thingness. Even though she may realize that her body is being exploited, she still feels that at least she is worth being used. The fulfilling contact of sex seems so much better to her than no-thingness.

Furthermore, it is pleasurable and fun to have one's body immersed in tingling eroticism. A person as body craves sex, for this

131

is what I am—a sexual being, and my sex can finally let me "be" and have fun at the same time. A person in the crisis of the limits may also be tempted to fulfill no-thingness with sex. He may be tempted to grasp something or someone rather than no-thing. This Don Juan can enjoy himself in the pleasure of sex rather than suffer in the pain of no-thingness.

Young adolescents who are experiencing negative no-thingness may also find sex a welcome relief. Here is something that makes sense and something that they can hold on to. Usually sex centers on solitary masturbation where they can stimulate and gratify their new and strong erotic desires without the threatening limits of reality. They can be fearless and perfect in their sexual fantasy world without being scared and limited. Masturbation offers them unlimited possibilities to explore sexual reality, for they can do anything in fantasy. The Other never says no, because the Other does what they want it to do. Older people may also masturbate, but usually for somewhat different reasons than those of the young adolescents. With older people, the decision to masturbate usually emerges from a "non-sexual" situation. Their masturbation is not linked to the satisfaction of newly found genital drives, but is frequently an escape from the pain of no-thingness.

Furthermore, my immediate and pre-reflective pleasure means that I do not have to think, but can let myself go. If I live from the neck up (theorism), I find the immediacy of sex a therapeutic experience, for I can come out of my theoretical world into the experiential world. I do not have to experience the world through the rubrics of technology, science, or language, but can experience it pre-reflectively. I can retreat from an abstract world of complex mediation to a concrete world of simple immediacy.

I also experience power in sexuality—the power of ecstasy,

the quiet power of being fulfilled and completed, the strength in being able to let go of oneself, and the potential power of creation are all present. When my power is not a spontaneous consequence of loving sex, my power is selfishly turned inward and becomes narcissistic. For example, a solitary masturbator has power in creating his fantasy world wherein he is the most powerful sexual being. Or a person may feel power in his ability "to make" the other. The man feels power in penetrating and satisfying the woman, and the woman feels powerful in being able to make the male become helpless in her arms.

Furthermore, too many men use their power in sexuality as a means of compensating for their inadequate sexual identity and fear of women. In their sexual exploits they feel powerful in being on top of the woman. Likewise, the woman's envy of man because of his control of the world is compensated for by her seduction and exploitation of the man. Therefore, both man and woman can gain a sense of power in different ways. In both cases, however, the striving for power in sex is usually a compensation for inferiority feelings toward one's own sex and toward the opposite sex.

I also experience a certain kind of ecstasy or quasi-transcendence in sexuality. I literally go out to and into the Other. If I am an advocate of theorism, I experience sex as a pleasant return to life; I begin to experience myself by going out of myself. I also experience ecstasy in that I am away from the routine of everyday life. Sex has no room for the tensions of everyday living, and it transcends normal time and place. The genital encounter is experienced as a timeless affair.

Sex also transcends the dichotomy between pleasure and pain, between joy and suffering. For instance, the partner's sounds in sex often attest to this unique and concrete paradox, at least insofar as it is difficult to distinguish between joy and suffering in the sexual climax. In a certain sense a person comes close to death in climax and at the same time feels most alive. He and she have spent themselves and yet feel most themselves.

Particularly in its initial encounters, sex has an almost unique relation to the holy experience. Its quasi-transcendence closely approximates the transcendence of a spiritual experience. The immediate fulfillment, completion, and actualization of sexuality give meaning to my life. In this sense, sex is a quasi-satisfaction of the transcendent movement of love. Nevertheless, even though I may initially try to love in some way, my love is not committed, long-lasting, and inclusive activity. Without love, my somatic and functional levels operate exclusively, and genitality becomes a substitute for love and therefore of the Holy. My fulfillment in sexualism is temporary and inadequate because sexuality needs the vitalization and support of love to make it last; otherwise, sexuality soon dissipates into onanistic behavior. Since the satisfaction of sex without love does not last, I must go back for more and more; I become a sex addict.

When I indulge in sexualism, I am selfish in that I unconsciously and/or consciously exploit the Other. My sexualism is not a concrete communication of love, not an affirmation and promotion of the Other. Neither does my behavior in corporate the world, but it is exclusive of it. Genital sex without love is an "inverse ratio" of the sexual fulfillment experienced in love. My sexualism becomes all-exclusive as contrasted to the all-inclusive fulfillment in loving sex. Sex without love makes "a world" the world; thus, it is selfish, not reality or Other-centered. Like the infant, I want, take, depend on, and suck off the Other. Thus, body-sex without self love becomes an inadequate fulfillment of no-thingness.

A significant aspect of sexuality is that its structure and function are creative and concrete. In promoting and leading to transcendence, fulfillment, and completion, genital sex calls for love and therefore commitment and responsibility. Consequently, in genital sex without love, I make an implied promise that is never fulfilled. This occurs because the nature of genital sex points to more than itself—to the promise of loving genital fulfillment. If I do not keep my promise, frustration and often consequent anger result. The woman especially feels this frustration, for it is her initial propensity to seek love and creation in sexuality. Furthermore, genital sex takes time and space, so that genital sex outside marriage simply becomes unwieldy. An unmarried person is forced to scheme as to how he or she will manage sex encounters. Thus, authentic sexuality is the unity of transcendency, space, and time that calls for a reliable situation of commitment and responsibility. This situation is generally called marriage. Conversely, genital sex without love is irresponsible and masturbatory.

When I displace love with sex, I am constantly searching for new bodies and thrills to satisfy desires. Fixation on the immediacy of sex forces me to find different bodies. I unconsciously search for the transcendent love in my exploits, but my futile attempts never find what I really need, because I ask sex to be the Holy.

If I do not run around from body to body or even if I do maintain my sex fixation, my sex orientation will eventually dissipate. Time and age prove decisive, so that the older I become, the less I can rely on sex. I have less energy, am less attractive, have less desire, and love calls me. It becomes increasingly difficult to satisfy myself through sex, and my search for the meaning of life in sex leaves me lifeless.

Sexualism means that my body, which I am, is made the ultimate. However, since my body is peripheral and temporary in its satisfaction, sex in itself is not enough. Only the Holy can satisfy my need for the Holy. Although sex may lead to love, love—not sex—leads me to the Holy.

Parenthetically, alcoholism and drug addiction are very similar to sexualism as displacements of the Holy. Alcohol is a popular and socially sanctioned escape from the loneliness of no-thingness and is particularly seductive for the dependent person. Like sex, alcohol offers the seduction of immediate pleasure and a temporary and selfish sense of well-being. While under the influence of alcohol, I do not worry about the demands of no-thingness and about the meaninglessness of existence.

The drug addict also goes on his problem-free trip. Getting and taking drugs become my ultimate concern, and everything and everyone is of secondary importance in reference to drugs. I feel few or no qualms even in exploiting my loved ones to get a "fix." Drug usage offers an instant escape frequently from personal and cultural theories. It enables me to break out of the bondage of ego processes and to plunge myself into the primacy of the body. Like sex, alcohol and drugs offer temporary and inadequate fulfillment of no-thingness.

LOVISM

Although love is the primary way to the human and holy Other, love can be used as a displacement of the Holy. "Lovism" means that I displace my desire for the Holy with an exclusive desire for the human Other. Since lovism includes a denial of the Holy, a

136

person's love becomes inauthentic.

A follower of lovism considers the Holy to be an interpersonal relationship, that is, love between humans exclusively. "God is love" means that love equals God, so that when two people love each other their love equals the Holy. In this orientation, life after death may be considered to be the person's heritage that I leave on earth primarily through love; thus, I live forever through my love acts.

Others may say that the Holy is social interest. Being the opposite of willpower, social interest incorporates an unconditional concern for others. When I reach a perfect state of social interest, I have then become the Holy. The Holy may also be considered as a symbol of our state of perfection, so that the Holy is man when he achieves the nirvana-like state of self-actualization.

The advocate of lovism usually functions primarily on the spiritual level. I try to live a life of love and tend to be highly critical of non-spiritual values such as technology and everyday living. I am ultrasensitive to spiritual and non-spiritual experiences, and I spontaneously differentiate between them. Honesty, authenticity, encounter, commitment, love, and freedom are paramount in my world; simple sincerity and presence is my way of living. Structure, establishment, inauthenticity, and solitude are words that are frowned upon. Love as a displacement for the holy is a very subtle deception, for the argument—God is love and love is God—contains much truth. However, this viewpoint is only partially correct.

We have already seen that love, the most perfect of human experiences, actualizes us and is the wellspring of wholeness and holiness. In love I promote the happiness and goodness of the Other for the Other's sake, and I become more of myself by giving myself in love. I discover that the meaningful order of love is an adequate answer to the meaningless chaos of no–thingness. In and through love I find the ground for a meaningful and actualizing life. In love life makes sense. Oh the other hand, we saw in Chapter 2 that love is an interpersonal relationship which should be oriented to people *and* to the Holy. Since authentic love includes both people and the Holy, the exclusion of one eventually destroys the other. I must love the Holy implicitly or explicitly in my love of others, but I must also be open for the holy encounter in solitude. The crucial point is that exclusive love of others is not a substitute for the love of the Holy. In fact, a denial of the personal transcendent in love with others or in solitude harms me and displaces the Holy.

The addict of lovism tends to live in a fantasy world in thinking that love is a panacea for everything. I may even try to love constantly, which is an impossible accomplishment, for I am not merely a loving being. Consequently I will fall apart or be extremely tired under the tension of love. I must realize that my body and ego are also valid and necessary modes of behavior and that my love must be implemented via my body and ego.

Love exclusive of the Holy, however, does make sense. Love movements, for instance, are often reactions against the inhuman behavior of the culture or of one's own environment. Groups are formed in order to practice the way of love without the inhumanness of the overall culture. Although participation in these groups can be a step in development, if promoted too long these groups tend to drift off into fantasy; that is, they have few ties with the common world. They forget that love must be implemented in the everyday, concrete world for it to be authentic. Whether the world is phony or not, it is still the real world. Otherwise, their love becomes exclusive, which is contrary to the nature of love. Dependent persons are prone to join these love groups, for like the child they need others to exist; consequently, they give love in order to receive love. Often they are still searching for the love they received or should have received as children. They depend too much on people and not enough on themselves and the Holy.

A person in lovism may also fall into a subtle form of masochism or sadism. The masochistic lover feels that he can get fulfillment from another person only by losing himself. I am willing to give myself to another at any cost, but my giving is for my own sake instead of for the Other. Since my meaning in life depends on other people, not on myself, my life is out of his control. Or, a person who must always be in control of love may become a sadistic lover. I cannot let go of myself, nor can I receive from the Other. Sometimes I fall into the "Jesus Christ syndrome" wherein I roam around giving love and blessings to those not so fortunate as I—usually to those weaker persons who depend on me. The masochist's love gives him or her a humble feeling of mammary satisfaction, and the sadist's love gives him or her a proud sense of virile security.

Other persons of lovism may be reacting against "solism" wherein I can experience the Holy only in solitude. Thus, solism is the opposite of lovism in that I reject the Holy in love encounters with people. In contrast to the advocate of lovism, I will eventually have to take a stand toward the Holy in his human relationships. If such a person opts to reject the presence of the Holy in inter-human relationships, his or her explicit love of the Holy in solitude will disintegrate.

The celibate mode of living particularly lends itself to this solistic displacement of the Holy. In this situation, instead of liberating a person for others and the Holy, celibacy is used as a means of withdrawal from the Other. The potential freedom of celibacy is perverted into a narcissistic escape from no-thingness. Living in a schizoid holy world, this schizoid celibate does not have to be concerned about the dynamics—the limits and potentials—of human relationships. On the other hand, some people react against this solistic approach and fall into lovism. For instance, a celibate woman, especially in her thirties, may see marriage as the only way for fulfillment. Marriage seductively offers her the convenient but temporary escape from the loneliness of no-thingness, and the new benefits of sex, children, and constant companionship are fulfilling. However, she fails to realize that if she cannot find herself in celibacy, she will probably be worse off in marriage. In some ways, a celibate person has to be healthier and holier than a married person, for a celibate lacks the immediate and gratifying benefits of marriage. However, since it is not so easy for a celibate to escape from no-thingness, the celibate can have a better opportunity to confront the Holy in and through no-thingness.

If a person in lovism does not reject the Holy, lovism in its early stages can be an immature but authentic response to no-thingness. For instance, it may be temporarily meaningful for a young woman to rebel against her inhuman view of God. If she has been taught about God merely in "supernaturalistic" terms, she may go to the opposite extreme and try to encounter God merely in "naturalistic" ways. She may see God only in human relationships exclusive of solitude. This humanism not only may be more meaningful than her past abstractionism, but it may eventually lead to more mature love—love that explicitly incorporates both the human and holy Other.

A humanist who lives in love without the explicit promotion of the Holy will usually come to a crisis. I will have to opt for or against the Holy. If I opt to be close to the Holy, my love for others will slowly dissipate; if I opt to be open to the Holy, my love for others will grow. Thus, the humanist's love can be a preparation for direct love of the Holy while being temporarily fulfilling and an adequate answer to no–thingness. However, if I reject the Holy, I will eventually get caught in the chaos of no–thingness, for only love of man and the Holy can save me from my no–thingness.

RELIGIONISM

The disciple of "religionism" tries to displace the Holy with inauthentic religion. Religionism can be the most subtle and dangerous displacement of the Holy, for it is done in the name of the Holy.

As a religionistic person I live according to a set system of religious behavior, and consequently follow a special form of theorism. I know the exercises for being religious, but I live the rule instead of living the holy life. I develop a safe and powerful way of living, for it seems that I always know the right way. There is no room for ambiguity and mystery. I eschew spiritual experiences of the Holy in favor of ego functions and experiences. I think, plan, and decide my religious life. I even think that I can tell other people exactly what to do in order to be holy. In converting or helping another, I use my ego motives of domination instead of my spiritual motives of appeal.

Rules, standards, and laws are necessary and have much value; but rules are fundamentally for life, not vice versa. These constructions of the ego make sense only when they are rooted in and are reflections of experiences. Rules can be incitive, not prescriptive. Rules do not tell a person exactly what to do, but they shed light and point the way. Instead of religious values and standards being rooted in experience, the advocate of religionism blindly submits to external rules, so that he or she is childish as a religious person.

A main reason for this legalistic dependency is that early in life a child is conditioned to follow certain "shoulds" and "should nots." A child is too young and dependent to explore the world and, more fundamentally, he or she has not reached the age of responsible freedom. However, too many adults carry these conditioned standards throughout life, and they try to live according to childish standards that are incongruent with their experience. Most of the standards are given to us by our culture primarily through our parents. Although these inherited standards are usually and basically true for the child and the parents, young adults must make them their own. The first positive experience of no—thingness brings a crisis of identity and intimacy that leads to our evaluation of these standards. These persons ask what is truth for them and they rebel against blind submission to past standards. They ask: How can I live my standards? How can my central motivation for living come from within? How can I become a person of conviction and commitment instead of a person of submission? Late adolescents want to live their lives and become true adults.

I may find that my standards and experiences are not in harmony, and I seek to find a way to have my standards promote life instead of repressing it. We have seen that I begin to doubt everything in the service of no–thing. I live the experiences of no–thingness, and it threatens many adults around me. Seldom am I given support, permission, and guidance to accept no–thingness, and I may be made to feel guilty for my doubt of religion. Through this pressure and my own inability to accept this situation, I may be seduced into accepting a "ready–made" religion, and consequently displace the Holy with religionism. I now experience the safety and power of religionism, and I enjoy the support and affirmation of the religionistic group—those people around me who also play the game of being holy. I become proud in knowing that I can look down on people in the name of the Holy, and yet I wonder why others resent me. In smug holiness I pray for them.

I become a caricature of a holy person. Although I go through all the motions, people know that I am acting. Slowly I become a hollow shell—rigid and brittle—so that when the voice of the Holy speaks to me in no–thingness, I may crumble. Those things—rules, standards, and laws—will no longer speak to me, but I am called to speak to things. I may not know that I must vitalize the rules, and that the rules will not vitalize me. If I find the Holy, others, and myself through no–thingness, then I will emerge to a mode of living wherein my standards are rooted within myself and in harmony with my unique personality. I will promote life, love, and encounter with the human and holy Other. My religious system will be a lived system. Otherwise, both my system and I will be lifeless.

SUMMARY

Our proposal has been that we displace the Holy in order to fulfill our no–thingness. Through our displacements we try to make sense of life and to be someone. We strive to find a ground for our existence—to find existential meaning in life. Theoretically, any object or activity can replace the Holy and be an inadequate response to our yearning for the Holy. Furthermore, if we try to displace the Holy with a substitute object, we will eventually alienate ourselves from others and from ourselves.

We conclude that love is the ground of our being—love for and from self, other, and the Holy. The Other is our hope of finding meaning in life, and we must have faith to experience the human and holy Other. Our experience of the Other saves us from our no-thingness, and this saving grace is love for and from the Other.

5 Healthiness and Holiness

WHAT IS HEALTHINESS? What is holiness? Are they the same? If not, how do they differ? What are their interrelations? In the light of our previous discussions and by way of summary, we respond to these issues.

A HEALTHY PERSON

One key feature of being healthy is that I actualize myself and the Other to the fullest possible degree without the impediments of psychological pathology and existential displacement. I realize and maintain an ongoing harmony of my three modes of existence. My body, ego, and spirit are vitally integrated and not at odds with one another. Knowing that all my modes of existence are necessary and meaningful interactions with reality, I do not sacrifice one system for the other. According to the situation, I behave in a way that is appropriate to my situation. For instance, if ego interaction is called for, I do not love explicitly, or if play is appropriate, I do not act in a task-oriented manner.

A healthy person, however, can never actualize all his or her potentiality, mainly because of structural, constitutional, cultural, and environmental factors. Since a person grows in degrees of healthiness, a child, for instance, cannot be as healthy as an adult. Or, identical twins may have the same genetic endowment, but because of their different environments the actualization of their potential may differ significantly. However, both persons may be healthy in that they actualized themselves in their situations—although in different ways and to various degrees. Our main point is that healthy persons are open to their experience of reality if and when it is possible.

As a healthy person I promote an availability to my body functions in listening to, accepting, admitting, and integrating the knowledge of my body. I am in tune with my own "expression" and I am sensitive to the expression of the Other. Since I, as a healthy person, value and I am present to the pre-reflective world of my body. Sexuality is important to me; I value being a man or a woman. I lack a schizoid or puritanical denial of my own and others' bodies and of the body at large—the world. Feelings, moods, and body interaction in general are an essential part of my humanity. I, furthermore, affirm my limits and admit that I am a being toward death. I also grow and become sensitive through my suffering.

I function in my ego mode when a situation elicits this behavior. I can usually work more fully and efficiently than the normal person. I do not have to be preoccupied with other things besides my job; I am free to work. I am also realistic in that I am open to reality and in that I learn how to implement ideas. My ego strength enables me to take charge of a situation and to distance myself from being seduced by trivia or from losing balance in sentimentality. Through ego functions I can communicate logically, explicitly, and publicly. Since my ego processes are oriented not only toward the world but also toward myself, I am able to integrate feelings, thoughts, and experiences. Finally, my ego reflects on my pre-reflective body and spiritual experiences and makes explicit sense of life.

The spiritual dimension is the core of a healthy person's motivative system. I become myself and discover the Other in and through my no-thingness. I do not displace the Other, but I opt for a ready availability to and for reality, and since I freely deter-

146

mine myself, I become the author of my existence. I am committed and have fundamental meaning in life, and my existence is grounded in love. In time, since I grow in openness, I become wise and childlike. Although I promote my body and ego, my spiritual experiences and values are most important to me. Love, understanding, acceptance, compassion, insight, responsibility, freedom, spontaneity, and zest for life betray my healthiness. I become more and more of myself by giving myself in love to the Other. I realize that I can actualize myself only by trying to actualize the Other.

I am happy and good. Since I live in harmony or at peace with myself and others, happiness permeates my existence. I am basically happy even when I confront personal problems or conflicts because I own up to what I am experiencing. I am also a good person in that I promote the emergence of life. My body, ego, and spirit love and celebrate life.

Whereas a healthy person grows into openness and out of closedness, an unhealthy person moves into closedness and out of openness. This person opts to be closed to certain experiences. For instance, if I repress my spiritual dimension in spite of the opportunity to actualize myself, I would be an unhealthy person. If I repress my emotional life, I would be attempting to disown what I am—an affective person. Since I am forced to lead a defensive and cautious life, I use much time and energy to frustrate the dynamic openness of myself. I am compelled to develop and repeat processes that repress, deny, and distort my unacceptable experiences. Furthermore, I am repeatedly compelled to use the Other to gratify my unsatisfied needs.

Unhealthiness is usually not a matter of willfulness or of free option, but is due most often to pre-reflective dynamics of which a person is unaware. Nevertheless, I pay the price for not letting myself be. I experience unhealthy anxiety, depression, restriction, somatic illness, tension, etc. My existence becomes a lived contradiction. I must be constantly careful not to let myself be.

Most people are neither healthy or unhealthy, but they try to lead a normal life of adequacy. Adequacy means to be barely sufficient, to satisfy the minimum demands of life. Being a normal person, I lead an adequate life in that I am able to meet the minimum demands of my life. However, I do not actualize the Other and myself to the fullest possible degree, nor do I live an orientation of love. I do just enough to maintain my life, particularly in the area of spiritual functions. This value of "just enough" is a symptomatic sign of normal people and its implementation—the coping mechanism of just enough—enables them to prevent mental illness.

The etymology of adequacy indicates that a person who lives an orientation of adequacy tries to equalize his or her needs to a state of equilibrium. In Freudian parlance, I strive for a comfortable state of equilibrium. For example, when I experience so-called signs of unhealthiness such as anxiety, depression, and tension, I immediately judge "it" as something to be gotten rid of by means of psychic or somatic repression. Since I fail to realize that these feelings are a manifestation of myself instead of an "it" to get rid of, I seldom accept and understand myself in my feelings.

Normal people live an adequate life to various degrees and for various reasons. Some people's primary concern is adequacy and their marginal existences are testimonies to their fundamental inadequacy. Others may lead adequate lives by investing too much energy in one realm and by which they displace the Holy. Still others move in and out of adequacy and frequently regress to adequacy when under stress. Some people realize that their lives are actually inadequate and they try to transcend their normalcy. Some succeed in their transcendence, but others never quite make it.

The reasons for a normal, adequate existence are many. Some immature persons never have had the opportunity to lead lives other than adequate ones. Furthermore, cultural and environmental forces often promote adequate modes of living. For instance, such strong cultural values as having rather than being, need gratification, technocracy, and the repression of spiritual experiences often promote adequacy. An adequate life can also be combined with unhealthiness, particularly neurosis, in that unconscious forces compel a person to live normally and unhealthily. And others may willfully opt to live the adequate life so that they gratify themselves at the expense of others.

R. D. Laing, a British psychiatrist who writes about the madness of normal people, is quite helpful in this context. Laing states that most people live out of their minds, that is, not in tune with their experiential lives. Since these people make up the majority of the population, this "formation" is usually presupposed to be authentic; but Laing questions the healthiness of this normal formation, pointing out that it may be a procrustean quagmire that incorporates a massive devastation of experience. He says that although these normal people are not ill in the traditional sense, they can be considered to be mad, for they are estranged from the most important experiences—those of authentic love, commitment, freedom, and openness. In short, this normal formation does not necessarily include the right way. Thus, a person who desires to live the way of authenticity must be somewhat out of the majority formation and consequently abnormal. (*The Politics of Experience*, pp. 81-82.)

The important point for this analysis is that a life of adequacy is normal but also mad, because it basically precludes a ready availability for and promotion of life—emergence—including myself and the Other. To do just enough, to satisfy the minimum demands of life is a form of madness. Although normal people submissively or unconsciously fall into the formation of the mad majority, healthy people freely opt to live in formation. They realize that actualization of self and the Other necessitates that they enter into the world of normal formation. They know that normalcy is also a dimension of their reality. However, healthy people also opt to go out of formation in order to find their way and yet they maintain a ready availability to implement their concerns in the formation of normalcy. Another kind of abnormal person— the holy person—is our next subject of discussion.

A HOLY PERSON

Although a description of the holy person has already been given in Chapter 2, particularly in terms of the consequent positive changes of the holy experience, the analysis did not include the constructs of no–thingness and displacement. For the sake of coherency and for its summary value, a succinct account of the holy person is presented and then used in comparing holy and healthy persons.

We have seen that a holy person lives according to the values and demands of the Holy. Since the Other in love is my ultimate concern, my central motivation is love. And although only a small part of my total life involves direct love—encounters with the Other—all my behavior is permeated with a holy orientation. As a holy person, my body and ego behavior disclose the Holy, and my spiritual experiences, especially those of love, proclaim the Holy. Thus, every action is in some way in service of the Holy.

Since I promote experiences of the Holy, my experiences of the world and others incorporate the numinous, the paradoxical, and the mysterious. I do not identify a person with his or her function, talent, or possessions, but I incorporate what persons are with what I can be. My faith and hope open me to the mystery of transcendence of the Other. My deeper penetration into reality lets me see the holy orientation of other persons even though they may be leading a displaced life.

Since I live in an orientation of holiness, I speak of the Holy. I am not constantly and explicitly preaching the message of the Holy, but neither am I embarrassed to speak of the Holy when it is appropriate. I am not scared and ashamed to talk of the very reality I stand for. When a situation calls for explicit discourse on the Holy, I have the courage to speak of the Holy even though I may be socially rejected. On the other hand, I never stop speaking of the Holy in implicit but very present terms, for my behavior is a radiation of the Holy.

The paramount sign of a holy person is love. I structure my life so that I can take time to love the Holy in solitude and with others. I am careful not to get caught in such displacements as workism so that I have little time for the Holy. In fact, all my activities are secondary priorities in regard to the Holy. Since my life is highly influenced by my transcendence in love to a sacred Other, I am not likely to be seduced by the profane, but I celebrate the profane in the light of love.

My life is also marked with existential indebtedness, guilt, worship, faith, and doubt. I am aware of my indebtedness to the human and holy Other, and my gratitude to the Other is expressed primarily in concrete manifestations of love. Besides enabling me to be constantly restless and unsatisfied (and yet I am at peace with these feelings), my existential guilt pushes me to grow into holiness. I also take time to worship in solitude and with others. Realizing the importance of my holy encounters, I worship with a certain humility and pride. My authentic worship sets me aside from the normal mode of living, yet I dare to be abnormal in standing up for the Holy. Finally, faith and doubt permeate my existence. I creatively accept and celebrate the numinous and I welcome doubt as an opportunity to go deeper into the Holy.

A holy person tends to be charismatic. My charisma does not necessarily mean that I have a dynamic personality, but that my holy orientation attracts and inspires people. People sense the presence of the Holy in me and they are inclined to listen to me. Others spontaneously want to know more about me as is shown in their respect for me.

Since a holy person lives in an orientation of love, I necessarily promote life. I do not harm or do violence to others, but I see others as brothers and sisters who are oriented toward each other and toward the Holy. I try to do what is best for the Other and I am willing to suffer for the Other's sake. I become a good person by doing good to others, and consequently I am moral. When the laws of morality are personalized, they become a matter of inner conviction. Even though I lead a good life, I am aware of the demon that lurks within me, and I openly affirm that my humanity includes the possibility of doing evil. By accepting and saying no to my evil inclinations, I grow more in goodness and farther away from evil.

Finally, as a holy person, I lead a meaningful life. I grow in and out of my no-thingness to a progressively deeper celebration of things, and I discover not only myself in no-thingness but also the Other. I do not displace the Other with substitute objects, but opt for the Holy as the ground of my existence. My love for and from the human and holy Other saves me from no-thingness and enables me to find my place in life. Since the Holy experiences are functions of my spirit, I am inclined to have other spiritual experiences such as wonder, beauty, and compassion. Although my life makes sense, I am not necessarily happy, for happiness involves being in basic harmony with oneself and the Other, and a person need not be in harmony in order to be holy. A holy person may be in unhealthy conflict because of factors that he or she cannot possibly cope with. This relation—healthiness and holiness—is the final topic of discussion.

A HEALTHY AND HOLY PERSON

Psychological health and holiness are related but are not identical. Since both healthy and holy persons live in love, they have ground and meaning in their existences. Love for and from the human and holy Other gives them meaning for being. Both persons also accept their no-thingness and actualize their spiritual modes of existence. Neither of them displaces the Other, but through their no-thingness they come to find their place in being with the Other. Thus, both the healthy and the holy person emerge out of no-thingness into a life that is motivated mainly by their spirit. However, there are differences between them.

First, consider healthy people in relation to holiness. It is quite possible to be healthy without direct worship of the Holy in that I love others but have not yet come to an explicit love of the Holy. Thus, I love the Holy implicitly in and through my relationships with others. If the Holy is not directly present to me, I find myself in a state of not-yetness. My not-yetness means that I experience an implicit presence to the Holy, but not yet an explicit one. Although healthy, I am somewhat immature in regard to my holiness.

Because of my orientation of openness and love, I will usually come to a confrontation with the Holy—to opt to accept or reject the Holy. The critical factor is that a healthy person does not reject the Holy or displace the Holy with a substitute object. If displacement does occur, then I am no longer healthy or whole, for I repress part of myself—my orientation toward the Other. If I opt to reject the Holy, I will become unhealthy, and if I opt to accept the Holy, I will begin to promote explicit holy encounters along with my implicit ones. I become a healthy and holy person.

Parenthetically, many people opt neither for nor against the Holy, but they try to lead a marginal existence with the Holy. They consider the Holy as one experience among many—not an experience of special and sacred import. These persons try to opt for the Holy especially in times of need, but tend to displace the Holy in times of plenty. These people maintain a normal relationship with the Holy.

Holiness, however, is no guarantee for healthiness. People may be holy but unhealthy. Many holy people are far from being models of mental health, yet they are good and holy people. Holy people may be unable to be open to or to integrate certain experiences because of past fixations, traumas, or repressions. For example, I may be unable to admit my feelings of hostility. Although I experience the Holy, I am closed to my hostility. Being holy and unhealthy, I do not willfully reject my experiences, but because of unconscious processes my freedom to opt for openness is curtailed. I lead a holy and good life, but not necessarily a happy one.

On the other hand, holiness may help me to endure and even make sense of my pathological pain. My love orientation enables me to accept my experiences, including the pathological. Thus, I am less likely to fight or repress my unhealthiness, but I am likely to transcend it. I find deeper meaning in my suffering. Holy and unhealthy people are basically happy, for they live with and transcend their suffering.

Nevertheless, holiness is not a magical panacea for unhealthiness. Although unhealthy functions do not preclude holy experiences, they may impede a fuller experience of the Holy. Since holy and unhealthy people are closed to dimensions of their experiences, they cannot fully involve themselves. In a sense, they are less than they could be when they present themselves to the Holy. Thus, a holy person should strive for psychological health, for it increases his or her availability to and for the Other. Holiness promotes wholeness, as does wholeness promote holiness. A holy person's availability to the Holy promotes openness to all his or her experiences, and a healthy person will be open in all areas.

A paramount point is that holiness is not synonymous with healthiness. A catchy phrase—"Holiness is wholeness"—can be just as atheistic as it is humanistic. Or, the phrase, "Divinization is humanization," can put the reality of God totally in the hands (personalities?) of human beings. People who live according to these assumptions tend to make healthiness their ultimate concern. Here, healthiness is a displacement for holiness. When I make healthiness my main value in life, I am likely to become too concerned in solving all my personal problems. I am inclined to focus too much on myself and not enough on the Other. When healthiness becomes my ultimate concern, life can become too easily an exercise in madness. Holiness is much more within my grasp precisely because it is beyond my grasp. The hope of humankind lies in holiness, not in healthiness.

The ideal is to be holy and healthy. We are open to and function appropriately in all our modes of existence. Our ultimate concern is love for and from self, others, and the Holy. Out of no—thingness and through love we find and become ourselves, and we bring love to the world and the world to love. Authentic persons have the freedom and courage to be out of normal formation and the commitment to celebrate abnormal concerns. Through a life of love, we become (w) hol (l) y.

~ ~ ~

Selected Bibliography

Aliport, Gordon W., *The Individual and His Religion*. The Macmillan Company, 1950.

Barth, Karl, *God Here and Now*, tr. by Paul M. van Buren. Harper & Row, Publishers, Inc., 1964.

Berdyaev, Nicolas, *The Divine and the Human*. London: Geoffrey Bles, Ltd., 1949.

Berger, Peter L., *The Sacred Canopy*. Doubleday & Company, Inc., 1967.

Boisen, A. T., *The Exploration of the Inner World*. Harper & Brothers, 1936.

Buber, Martin, *I and Thou*, tr. by Ronald Gregor Smith. 2d ed. Charles Scribner's Sons, 1958.

Cummings, Charles. *Spirituality and the Desert Experience*. Dimensions Books, 1978.

De Lubac, Henri, *The Discovery of God*. P. J. Kenedy & Sons, Publishers, 1960.

Doerff, Frances, *The Art of Passing Over*. Paulist Press, 1988.

Eliade, M., *The Sacred and the Profane*. Harper Torch Books, 1959.

Ferguson, Kitty. *The Fire in the Equations: Science, Religion, and the Search for God*. William B. Eerdmons Publishing Co., 1994.

Feuerbach, Ludwig. *The Essence of Christianity*, tr. by George Eliot. Harper & Brothers, 1957.

Franki, Viktor E., *The Doctor and the Soul: An Introduction to Logotherapy*. Alfred A. Knopf, Inc., 1955.

Freud, Sigmund, *Civilization and Its Discontents*, ed. and tr. by James Strachey. W. W. Norton & Company, Inc., 1961.

Freud, Sigmund, *The Future of an Illusion*. Doubleday & Company, Inc., Anchor Books, 1964.

Goldbrunner, Josef, *Holiness Is Wholeness and Other Essays*. University of Notre Dame Press, 1964.

Heidegger, Martin, *Being and Time*, tr. by John Macquarrie and Edward Robinson. Harper & Brothers, 1962.

Heschel, Abraham J., *Who Is Man?* Stanford University Press, 1965.

Hocking, William Ernest, *The Meaning of God in Human Experience*. Yale University Press, 1912.

James, William, *The Varieties of Religious Experience*. The New American Library, Mentor Books, 1958.

Jaspers, Karl, and Bultmann, Rudolf, *Myth and Christianity*. The Noonday Press, 1958.

Jones, Christopher. *A Meditation on Suffering and Helplessness*. Templegate Publishers, 1978.

Jung, C. G., *Modern Man in Search of a Soul*, tr. by C. F. N Baynes. Harcourt, Brace & World, Inc., 1995

Jung, C.G., *The Undiscovered Self*, tr. by R. F. C. Hull, New American Library, Mentor Books, 1959

Jung, C.G., *Psychology and Religion*, tr. by R. F. C. Hull. Pantheon Books, Inc., 1958.

Jurji, Edward J., *The Phenomenology of Religion*. The Westminster Press, 1963.

Kraft, William F., *A Psychology of Nothingness*. The Westminster Press, 1973.

Kraft, William F., *Normal Modes of Madness*. Alba House, 1978.

Kraft, William F., *Whole and Holy Sexuality*, Abbey Press, 1989.

Kung, Hans, *The Unknown God?* Sheed & Ward, Inc., 1966.

Kwant, Remy C., *Encounter*, tr. by Robert C. Adolfe. Duquesne University Press, 1960.

Laing, R. D., *Politics of Experience*. Pantheon Books, Inc., 1967.

Lawrence, Brother. *The Practice of the Presence of God*. Whitaker House, 1982

Lepp, Ignace, *Atheism in Our Time*. The Macmillan Company, 1963.

Luckmann, Thomas, *The Invisible Religion*. The Macmillan Company, 1967.

Luijpen, William A., *Phenomenology and Atheism*. Duquesne University Press, 1964.

Luijpen, William A., *Existential Phenomenology*, tr. by Henry J. Koren, Duquesne University Press, 1964.

Maloney, George. *On The Road to Perfection. Christian Humility in Modern Society*, New City Press, 1995.

Marcel, Gabriel, *Problematic Man*. Herder and Herder, Inc., 1967.

Maslow, A. H., *Toward a Psychology of Being*. Van Nostrand Company, Inc., 1962.

Maslow, A. H., *Religion, Values, and Peak-Experiences*, Ohio State University Press, 1964.

May, Gerald G., *Addiction and Grace*. Harper Row, 1989.

Moore, Thomas, Verner, *The Life of Man with God*. Doubleday & Company, Inc., Image Books, 1962.

Moore, Thomas, *Care of the Soul*. HarperCollins, 1992.

Moustakas, Clark, *Loneliness*. Prentice-Hall, Inc., Spectrum Books, 1961.

Mowrer, O. Hobart, *The Crisis in Psychiatry and Religion*. D.

Van Nostrand Company, Inc., 1961.

O'Dea, Thomas F., *The Sociology of Religion.* Prentice-Hall, Inc., 1966.

Otto, Rudolf, *The Idea of the Holy.* Oxford University Press, Galaxy Books, 1958.

Otto, Rudolf, *Mysticism East and West.* Collier Books, 1960.

Padovano, Anthony T., *The Estranged God.* Sheed & Ward, Inc., 1966.

Pahnke, Walter N., and Richards, William A., "Implications of LSD and the Experience of Mysticism," *Journal of Religion and Health,* Vol. V., No.3 (July, 1966), pp. 175-188.

Rahner, Karl, *The Christian Commitment,* tr. by Cecily Hastings. Sheed & Ward, Inc., 1963.

Robinson, John A. T., *Honest to God.* The Westminster Press, 1963.

Rümke, H. D., *The Psychology of Unbelief.* Sheed & Ward, Inc., Canterbury Books, 1962.

Salinger, J. D., *The Catcher in the Rye.* Little, Brown and Company, 1945.

Sartre, Jean-Paul, *Being and Nothingness,* tr. by Hazel E. Barnes. Philosophical Lib., Inc., 1956.

Scheler, Max, *Man's Place in Nature,* tr. by Hans Meyerhoff. The Noonday Press, 1961.

Schielermacher, Friedrich, *The Christian Faith,* Vol. I. Harper & Row, Publishers, Inc., 1963.

Teilhard de Chardin, Pierre, *The Divine Milieu.* Harper & Row, Publishers, Inc., 1960.

Teresa of Avila. *The Collected Works of St. John of the Cross.* tr. Kieran Kavanaugh and Otilio Rodriquez, ICS Publication, 1973.

Teresa of Avila. *The Interior Castle.* tr. Kieran Kavanaugh and Otilio Rodriquez, Paulist Press, 1979.

Thouless, Robert H., *An Introduction to the Psychology of Religion.* London: Cambridge University Press, 1961.

Tillich, Paul, *The Courage to Be.* Yale University Press, 1952.

Tillich, Paul, *Dynamics of Faith.* Harper Torch-Books, 1957.

Underhill, Evelyn, *Mysticism: A Study in the Nature and Development of Man's Spiritual Consciousness.* E. P. Dutton & Company, Inc., 1911.

Underhill, Evelyn, *Practical Mysticism.* E. P. Dutton & Company, Inc., 1915.

Underhill, Evelyn, *The Mystics of the Church.* Schocken Books, Inc., 1964.

Van Croonenburg, Bert, *Gateway to Reality.* Duquesne University Press, 1965.

Van der Leeuw, G., *Religion in Essence and Manifestation.* 2 vols. Harper & Row, Publishers, Inc., 1963.

Van Kaam, Adrian, *Religion and Personality.* Prentice-Hall, Inc., 1964.

Van Kaam, Adrian, *Existential Foundations of Psychology.* Duquesne University Press, 1966.

Wach, Joachim, *Types of Religious Experience, Christian and Non-Christian.* The University of Chicago Press, 1951.

Wallace, Anthony F. C., *Religion: An Anthropological View.* Random House, Inc., 1966.

Watts, Alan W., *Nature, Man and Woman.* The New American Library, 1960.

Weber, Max, *The Sociology of Religion.* Beacon Press, Inc., 1964.

Weigel, Gustave, *The Modern God.* The MacmillanCompany, 1959.

Well, Simone, *Waiting for God*, tr. by Emma Craufurd. G. P. Putnam's Sons, 1951.

White, Victor, Or. P., *God and the Unconscious*. The World Publishing Company, 1952.

Whitehead, Alfred North, *His Reflections on Man and Nature*, ed. by Ruth Nanda Anshen. Harper & Brothers, 1961.

WILLIAM F. KRAFT

is a graduate of Duquesne University, and has been the chief of psychology at psychiatric hospitals and an adjunct professor at the Institute of Formative Spirituality. Dr. Kraft is a professor of psychology at Carlow College, maintains a part-time private practice, publishes extensively, and is a national and international speaker. He is married to Pat, and is the proud father of Jennifer and Bill.